I0458324

Words of Muslim Wisdom

Compiled by
Gregory Heary

Umar bin al Khattab said:

"There is no goodness in people who don't give advice, and there is no goodness in people who don't like to be advised."

Risaalat Al Mustarshideen, 71

Umar bin Al-Khattab said:

"Whoever decorates himself by displaying to the people some characteristics that Allah knows are contrary to his real characteristics, will be disgraced and dishonored by Allah."

Ad-Daaraqutnee, 4/207

Imam Al-Awzaa'ee (d.157) said:

"Make yourself patient upon the Sunnah, stop where the people stopped, speak with what they spoke with, and refrain from what they refrained from. And follow the path of your Righteous Predeccessors (Salafus Saaliheen) for verily, sufficient for you is that which was sufficient for them."

Ash-Sharee'ah by Al-Aajurree p.58

Fudayl ibn Iyad said:

"Whoever marries his beloved daughter to an innovator has cut off the ties of relationship with her."

Al-Barbaharee, An Explanation of the Creed 137

It is reported that Muʿāwiyah bin Qurrah said:

"Do not sit with the foolish using your knowledge, and do not sit with the knowledgeable (scholars) using your foolishness."

Al-Dhahabī, Siyar Aʿlām Al-Nubalāʾ 5:154.

It is reported that Sufyān Al-Thawrī said:

"Safety lies in not wanting to be known."

Al-Dhahabī, Siyar Aʿlām Al-Nubalāʾ 7:258

It is reported that Qatādah said:

"Verily the Qurān guides you to your disease and your treatment: as for your disease, it is your sins; and as for your treatment, it is to seek the forgiveness of Allāh."

Al-Bayhaqī, Shuʿab Al-Īmān 9:347 no. 6745.

It is reported that ʿAbdullāh bin Al-Mubārak said:

"The seeking of knowledge cannot really be achieved except with four things: time (al-farāgh, being free to study), sufficient wealth (al-māl, to avoid preoccupation with seeking a living), preservation (al-ḥifẓ, memorization) and piety (al-waraʿ, religious cautiousness)."

Al-Bayhaqī, Shuʿab Al-Īmān 3:243, article 1602.

It is reported that Abū Ḥāzim Salamah bin Dīnār said:

"You cannot be a scholar unless you have three traits: you do not transgress against those above you, you do not look down on those lesser than you, and you do not take any dunyā in return for your knowledge."

Al-Bayhaqī, Shuʿab Al-Īmān 3:282, article 1655.

It is reported that ʿUmar bin Al-Khaṭṭāb said to a young man while exhorting him:

"A man might have ten qualities, nine of them good and one bad, but the nine good ones can be spoiled by the one bad quality. Beware of the slips and faults of youth."

ʿAbd Al-Razzāq Al-Ṣanʿānī, Al-Muṣannaf 8240.

It is reported that ʿAbdullāh bin Al-Mubārak said:

"The insightful and wise do not trust that they are safe from four things: a past sin about which it is not known what the Lord Almighty will do, the remaining lifespan wherein it is not known what destruction lies, some (apparent) advantage a person is given but which could be a lure (from Allāh) in recompense for his wrongdoing, a misguidance that has been beautified – so that he thinks it is guidance – and a momentary deviation of the heart, for a person can be stripped of his religion without realizing it."

Al-Dhahabī, Siyar Aʿlām Al-Nubalāʾ 8:406.

Yūnus reports: Maymūn bin Mihrān once wrote to me saying:

"Beware of dispute and argumentation about the religion, and do not argue with a scholar nor an ignoramus. As for the scholar, he will withhold his knowledge from you, and will not be concerned with what you do. As for the ignorant person, he will only cause roughness in your heart and he will not obey you [anyway]."

Al-Dārimī, Al-Sunan no. 302.

It is reported that Sufyān Al-Thawrī said:

"I have not seen less zuhd (abstinence) in anything than leadership; you can see a man renouncing food, drink, wealth

and clothing, but if his leadership is contested, he vehemently defends and has enmity over it."

Al-Dhahabī, Siyar ʾAʿlām Al-Nubalāʾ 7:262.

It is reported that Al-Ḥasan Al-Baṣrī said:

"Whoever is happy (satisfied) with what Allāh has apportioned for him, it will suffice him and Allāh will bless it for him, but whoever is not satisfied, then [what is apportioned for him] will not suffice him and it will not be blessed."

Ibn Abī Al-Dunyā, Kitāb Al-Riḍā ʿan Allāh bi Qaḍāʾihi article 95

Saʿīd bin Abī ʿArūbah said:

"Whoever has not heard the differences of opinion, then do not consider him a scholar."

Ibn ʿAbd Al-Barr, Jāmiʿ Bayān Al-ʿIlm wa Faḍlihī no. 1521.

It is reported that Ayyūb Al-Sakhtiyānī said:

"A man does not become noble until he has two qualities: he is undesirous of what other people possess, and he pardons and overlooks them."

Ibn Ḥibbān, Rawḍatu Al-ʿUqalāʾ p167.

It is reported that Al-Ḥasan Al-Baṣrī said:

"A man remains upon good as long as he knows what things spoil his deeds."

Aḥmad bin Ḥanbal, Al-Zuhd p339.

ʿAlī bin Abī Ṭālib said:

"Do not be from those who are hasty, who broadcast (what should not be broadcast), who plant trouble by divulging what should be secret, for you will face severe, prolonged and heavy tribulations."

Al-Bukhārī, Al-Adab Al-Mufrad no. 327. Its chain of transmission was graded ṣaḥīḥ by Al-Albānī in Ṣaḥīḥ Al-Adab Al-Mufrad no.250.

ʿAbdullāh bin Masʿūd said:

"The victim of theft might continue to suspect and conjecture [about who stole from him] until he becomes worse [in sin] than the thief."

Al-Bukhārī, Al-Adab Al-Mufrad no. 1289. Its chain of transmission was graded ṣaḥīḥ by Al-Albānī in Ṣaḥīḥ Al-Adab Al-Mufrad no.974.

ʿAbdullāh bin ʿAwn said:

"There are three things that I like for myself and for my brothers: That the Muslim man looks to the Qurān; he learns it, recites it, ponders it and refers to it. Second, that he looks to the narrations and the Sunnah; he asks about it and follows it with all his efforts. Third, that he leaves alone all these people except when doing good."

Al-Bukhāri, Al-Ṣaḥīḥ, no. 97 (in annotative, discontiguous form). The chain of transmission is connected in Al-Marwazī, Al-Sunnah, no. 108.

It is reported that Bilāl bin Saʿd said:

"A brother who, whenever you meet him, points out to you one of your faults (for you to correct yourself) is better for you than a brother who, whenever you meet him, puts a dīnār (money) in your hand."

Abū Bakr Al-Daynūrī, Al-Mujālasah wa Jawāhir Al-ʿIlm no. 1428.

It is reported that Abū Bakr Al-Ṣiddīq said:

"Beware of lying, for lying is far removed from īmān(faith)."

Abū Bakr Al-Ḵallāl, Al-Sunnah no. 1467, 1470; Al-Bayhaqī, Shuʿab Al-Īmān no. 4463.

It is reported that ʿAlī bin ʾAbī Ṭālib said:

"Do not be with the sinner (fājir), for he will beautify to you the things he does, and he will want you to be like him; and he will beautify to you the worst of his practices; and his entrance upon you and leaving from your company will cause ignominy and discredit [of you]. And do not accompany the fool (aḥmaq), for he will exhaust himself [to help you] but will not benefit you, and he may want to benefit you but end up harming you; his silence is better than his speaking, his distance is better than his closeness, and him dying is better than him living. And do not accompany the liar, for life will not benefit you with him, he will tell others what you say, and tell you what others say; and if you speak the truth, it will not be believed."

Abū Bakr Al-Daynūrī, Al-Mujālasah wa Jawāhir AlʿIlm no. 1379.

It is reported that Yaḥyā bin Abī Kathīr said:

"It used to be said, "People have never honoured themselves with anything [better] than the obedience of Allāh, and they have never dishonoured themselves with anything [worse] than disobedience to Allāh.""

Ibn Abī Al-Dunyā, Muḥāsabatu Al-Nafs article 98.

It is reported that Abū Ḥāzim Salamah bin Dīnār was once asked:

"O Abū Ḥāzim, do you not see how prices have risen?" He replied, "And what is the worry? Verily, he (Allāh) who provides for us during deflation is the one who will provide for us during inflation."

Abū Nuʿaym, Ḥilyatu Al-ʾAwliyāʾ 3:239.

It is reported that Al-Shaʿbī said:

"Stay away from the sinful amongst the scholars and the ignorant amongst the worshippers, for these two are the calamity of everyone who would fall into fitnah."

Al-Bayhaqī, Shuʿab Al-Īmān ḥadīth 1753.

It is reported that Al-Fuḍayl bin ʿAyyād said:

"There is no one who loves authority (leadership) except that he envies, transgresses, chases the faults of others and dislikes anyone being mentioned in a good light."

Ibn ʿAbd Al-Barr, Jāmiʿ Bayān Al-ʿIlm article. 971.

It is reported that Saʿīd bin Jubayr said:

"Verily, fear (al-khashyah) is that you fear Allāh such that your fear comes between you and your disobedience (of Allāh). That is

khashyah. And dhikr (remembrance) is obedience to Allāh: whoever obeys Allāh has remembered Him; and whoever does not obey Him is not a rememberer of Him, even if he says a lot of tasbīḥ and recites a lot of Qurān."

Al-Dhahabī, Siyar ʾAʿlām Al-Nubalāʾ 4:326.

It is reported that Sufyān Al-Thawrī said:

"Whoever takes leadership quickly (too early) will harm a lot of [his] knowledge (will not learn what he needs); and whoever does not take leadership can continue to seek knowledge until he reaches [where he needs to be]."

Al-Dārimī, Al-Sunan #554.

It is reported from Ḥabīb Al-Jallāb that he asked ʿAbdullāh bin Al-Mubārak :

"What is the best thing a person is ever given?" He replied, "Innate intelligence." He then asked, "And if not that?" He replied, "Good conduct." He then asked, "And if not that?" He replied, "A compassionate brother to consult." He then asked, "And if not that?" He replied, "Long silence." He asked, "And if not that?" Ibn Al-Mubārak replied, "Then an early death."

Al-Dhahabī, Siyar ʾAʿlām Al-Nubalāʾ 8:397.

Ayyūb Al-Sakhtiyānī reports that Abū Qilābah said:

"O Ayyūb, when Allāh brings about knowledge for you, bring about worship of him, and do not let your [sole] concern be to narrate it."

Ibn ʿAbd Al-Barr, Jāmiʿ Bayān Al-ʿIlm, article 1279.

It is reported that Ibrāhīm bin Adham said:

"Whoever seeks knowledge sincerely, for the servants of Allāh to benefit by and to benefit himself, then being hidden (from fame) is more beloved to him than seeking loftiness. He is the one who becomes more lowly to himself, strives more in worship, fears Allāh more, yearns for Allāh more, and becomes more humble amongst people. He cares not what he has of this dunyā night or day."

Al-Bayhaqī, Shuʿab Al-Īmān article 1653.

It is reported that Al-Zuhrī said to Yūnus bin Yazīd:

"O Yūnus! Do not try to overcome knowledge, for verily knowledge is [like vast] valleys: whichever of them you take will stop you before you traverse it. Instead, take it over the days and nights. And do not take knowledge all at once, for whoever tries to take it all at once will lose it all at once. Rather take it bit by bit over the days and nights."

Ibn ʿAbd Al-Barr, Jāmiʿ Bayān Al-ʿIlm article 652.

It is reported that Abū Al-Dardā' said:

"When you adorn your copies of the Qurān and embellish your mosques, destruction will be upon you."

Ibn Al-Mubārak, Al-Zuhd wa Al-Raqā'iq, article 746. Shaykh Al-Albānī stated that the chain of transmission of this narration consists of reliable reporters, except he did not know if the reporter Bakr bin Suwādah had heard directly from Abū Al-Dardā'. The narration corroborates a similar ḥadīth reported from the Prophet himself. See Al-Ṣaḥīḥah ḥadīth 1351.

It is reported that Al-ʿAwwām bin Ḥawshab said:

"Boasting that you did a sin (when you did not) is worse than committing the sin."

Al-Daynūrī, Al-Mujālasah wa Jawāhir Al-ʿIlm, article 3073.

It is reported that Bakr bin ʿAbdillāh Al-Muzanī said:

"When you see someone older than you, say: he has preceded me in īmān and righteous actions so he is better than me; and when you see someone younger than you, say: I have preceded him in sinning and disobedience so he is better than me. And when you see your brothers honouring and revering you, say: this is a virtue they have attained; and when you see them falling short (in their treatment of you) say: this is [because of] a sin I committed."

Ibn Al-Jawzī, Ṣifatu Al-Ṣafwah, article 505: Bakr bin ʿAbdillāh Al-Muzanī.

It is reported that ʿAbdullāh bin Masʿūd said:

"Do not be hasty in praising people or blaming them, for perhaps what pleases you from a person today will displease you tomorrow, and perhaps what displeases you today, will please you tomorrow. Indeed, people change. It is Allāh who forgives the sins. And Allāh is more merciful to his servant the day he meets him than a mother who lays out a bed for her child in an empty patch of land and feels [the ground]: if there is a risk of being stung, it will be her instead of him (her child), and if there is a risk of being pricked by a thorn, it will be her instead of him."

Al-Bayhaqī, Shuʿab Al-Īmān article 6177, and others.

ʿAbdullāh bin Masʿūd said:

"The people will not cease to be well as long as they take knowledge from their seniors. When they take it from their juniors and their bad people, they will be destroyed."

Ibn ʿAbd Al-Barr, Jāmiʿ Bayān Al-ʿIlm article 1057.

It is reported ʿAbdullāh bin Al-ʿAmr bin Al-ʿĀṣ said:

"Nifāq (hypocrisy) used to be something unusual amongst all the Īmān(faith). Soon, Īmān will be something strange amongst all the nifāq."

Ibn Baṭṭah, Al-Ibānah 1:173 article 6.

It is reported that Al-Ḥasan Al-Baṣrī said:

"Do not sit with the people of desires (Bidʿah, heresy), even if you think you have a response [to what they say]."

Al-Harawī, Dhamm Al-Kalām article 765.

ʿAbbād bin Al-ʿAwwām narrates:

Sharīk bin ʿAbdillāh came to us around fifty years ago, and we said to him, "O Abū ʿAbdillāh, here amongst us there are people from the Muʿtazilah who reject these āḥādīth [like]: 'Allāh descends to the lowest heaven', and 'the people of Jannah will see their Lord'. So Sharīk narrated to me around ten such narrations, then said: 'As for us, we have taken our religion from the sons of the Tābiʿīn, from the Ṣaḥābah. Who have they taken from?'"

Al-Ḏahabī, Al-ʿUluw. Graded ṣaḥīḥ by Al-Albānī in Mukhtaṣar Al-ʿUluw article 146.

It is reported that Muʿlā bin Al-Faḍl said:

"They (the Salaf) used to supplicate to Allāh for six months asking Him to get them to the month of Ramaḍān; and they used to supplicate for six months that Allāh accept [their fasting and other worship in Ramaḍān]."

Abul-Qāsim Al-Aṣbahānī, Al-Targhīb wa Al-Tarhīb article 1761.

It is reported that Sufyān Al-Thawrī said:

"Knowledge is only learned to [apply it and] put into practice the Taqwā of Allāh the mighty and sublime."

Abū Bakr Al-Daynūrī, Al-Mujālasah wa Jawāhir Al-ʿIlm article 943.

Anas bin Mālik reports:

"A young man who had stolen was brought to ʿUmar (for punishment). He said, "By Allāh I have never stolen before this time." So ʿUmar responded, "You lie, Allāh would not (or does not) surrender a servant of His on the first sin.""

Abū Dāwūd, Al-Zuhd article 56, and others. Graded ṣaḥīh by Ibn Kathīr and others.

It is reported that Ḥudhayfah was asked:

""What is the worst fitnah?" He replied, "That good and evil is presented to you and you do not know which of them to follow.""

Ibn Abī Shaybah, Al-Muṣannaf, Kitāb Al-Fitan, article 38565.

It is reported that Al-Ḍaḥḥāk bin Muzāḥim, the famous scholar of tafsīr from the Tābiʿīn, said:

"No one who has learned Qurān and then forgotten it except due to a sin he has committed, because Allāh the most high said:

وَمَآ أَصَـٰبَكُم مِّن مُّصِيبَةٍ فَبِمَا كَسَبَتْ أَيْدِيكُمْ

Qurān 42:30

"And no calamity befalls you except due to what your own hands have earnt."

And forgetting the Qurān is one of the greatest calamities."

Al-Bayhaqī, Shuʿab Al-Īmān article 1813, and others.

Muḥammad bin Sīrīn said:

"A man amongst the Companions of the Prophet would go three days without finding anything to eat, so he would take some animal skin, roast it and eat that. If he found nothing at all, he would tie a rock to himself to straighten his back."

Al-Mundhirī, Al-Tarġīb wa Al-Tarhībin Graded ḥasan by Al-Albānī. See Ṣaḥīḥ Al-Tarġīb wa Al-Tarhīb article 3310.

It is reported from ʿAbdullāh bin ʿUmar:

When ʿUmar bin Al-Khaṭṭāb arrived in Al-Shām, he said to Abū ʿUbaydah: "Take us to your home." Abū ʿUbaydah said, "And what will you do with my home?" ʿUmar replied, "Just take us there." Abū ʿUbaydah said, "You only want to cry your eyes out over me." So he entered his house and saw nothing [by way of furnishings] in it. ʿUmar asked, "Where are your things? I see nothing but rags, a water-skin and a dish (tray), and you are a governor! Do you have food?" So Abū ʿUbaydah went over to an old pail (bucket) and took out some scraps, and ʿUmar began to weep. Abu ʿUbaydah said to him, "I told you you would cry your eyes out over me. O Commander of the Believers, sufficient for you from the dunyā is what delivers you to your place of rest." 'Umar said, "The dunyā changed us all except you Abū 'Ubaydah."

Abū Dāwūd, Kitāb Al-Zuhd article 123, and others.

Whenever ʿAbdullāh bin ʿAbbās saw a muṣḥaf (copy of Qurān) decorated with silver or gold he would say:

"Do you tempt the thief, when its beauty is in its inside?"

Abū ʿUbayd Al-Qāsim bin Sallām, Faḍāʾil Al-Qurān article 907.

It is reported that ʿAlī bin Abī Ṭālib said:

"Blessings arrive with gratitude [to Allāh], and gratitude is connected with more [blessings], and the two are tied together: more blessings from Allāh will never stop unless gratitude from the servant stops."

Ibn Abī Al-Dunyā, Al-Shukr article 18.

It is reported that ʿAbd Al-ʿAzīz bin Abī Rawwād said to a man:

"Whoever does not take exhortation [and is not effected] by three things, will not be exhorted by anything: Islām, the Qurān and old age (graying)."

Ibn Abī Al-Dunyā, Al-ʿUmr Wa Al-Shayb #40

It is reported that Imām Mālik said:

"The Salaf used to teach their children to love Abū Bakr and 'Umar like they used to teach them a sūrah of the Qurān."

Al-Lālakāʾī, Sharḥ ʾUsūl ʾIʿtiqād Ahl Al-Sunnah #2325.

Abū ʾUmāmah said:

"Verily Shayṭān comes to your bed after your wife has made it and prepared it and throws a stick, a stone, or something [similar] on it to make the husband angry with his wife. So if someone finds this, let him not be angry with his wife, for it is the work of Shayṭān."

Al-Bukhārī, Al-Adab Al-Mufrad #1191.

It is reported that Maymūn bin Mihrān said:

"There are three things that must be given to both the righteous and the sinful: the ties of the womb (relatives) must be kept connected, whether they are righteous or sinful; trust must be fulfilled, for the righteous and the sinful; and promises must be kept, to the righteous as well as the sinful."

Ibn Abī Shaybah, Al-Muṣannaf 12:298.

It is reported that ʿAlī [bin Abī Ṭālib] said:

"The masājid are the sittings of the Prophets, and a protection from Shayṭān."

Al-Ḵaṭīb, Al-Jāmiʿ li-ʾAḵlāq Al-Rāwī #1200.

It is reported that Muḥammad Ibn Sīrīn said:

"We were once in the house of ʿAlqamah bin Qays. Rabīʿ bin Ḵuthaym entered upon us and sat in a corner of the house. Then he said, "Speak only a little except for nine things: subḥānallāh, al-ḥamdulillāh, lā ilāha illallāh, Allāhu ʾakbar, reciting the Qurān, enjoining good, forbidding wrong, asking Allāh for what is good and seeking His protection from harm (evil).""

Hannād bin Al-Sarīy, Al-Zuhd #1108.

Bilāl bin Saʿd – Allāh have mercy him – said:

"When a sin is hidden it harms only the perpetrator, but if it is made apparent and not rectified, it harms all the people."

Ibn Waḍḍāḥ, Al-Bidʿah #287.

It is reported that Khālid bin Maʿdān said:

"Whoever seeks praise by [saying or doing] what goes against Allāh, Allāh will turn those praises back on him to blame; and whoever is bold enough to [say or do] what brings blame [from people but] is in conformity to the truth, Allāh will turn that blame into praise."

Abū Dāwūd, Al-Zuhd #494.

It is reported that Jābir bin ʿAbdullāh said:

"Have taqwā of Allāh and behave modestly (with a sense of shame), and cover yourselves; let not any of you bathe except behind a covering."

Al-Bayhaqī, Shuʿab Al-Īmān #7398.

It is reported that ʿAṭā bin Abī Rabāḥ said:

"Sometimes a man narrates a ḥadīth to me, so I remain quiet as if I am listening carefully, although I had heard the ḥadīth before he had even been born."

Al-Ḏahabī, Siyar Aʿlām Al-Nubalāʾ 5:87.

It is reported that Al-Layth [bin Saʿd] said:

"I used to walk with Ṭalḥah, and he [once] said, "If I knew that you were older than me by even one night, I would never walk in front of you.""

Abū Nuʿaym, Ḥilyatu Al-Awliyāʾ 5:17.

It is reported that Imām Al-Shāfiʿī said:

"Do not live in a land in which there is neither a scholar to inform you about your religion, nor a doctor to tell you about your body."

Al-Bayhaqī, Manāqib Al-Shāfiʿī 2:115

ʿAmr bin Dīnār reports that ʿAbdullāh bin ʿUmar intended not to marry after the [passing of the] Prophet, so Ḥafṣah (his sister) advised him:

"My brother, marry, for if you have a child and it dies, it will precede you into Al-Jannah (and be a cause for you to be admitted), and if it lives, the child will supplicate for good for you."

ʿAbd Al-Razzāq Al-Ṣanʿānī, Al-Muṣannaf #10388

A man once asked ʿAbdullāh bin ʿAmr bin Al-ʿĀṣ:

"Are we not from the poor of the Muhājirīn?" He replied, "Do you have a wife to go back to?" The man replied, "Yes." ʿAbdullāh asked, "Do you have a home to live in?" The man said, "Yes." ʿAbdullāh said, "Then you are one of the rich." The man said, "And I have a servant." ʿAbdullāh said, "In that case, you are a king!"

Muslim, Al-Ṣaḥīḥ #5290

It is reported that ʿAbdullāh bin Masʿūd said:

"If the people were gathered on one plain, all of them believers, except for two unbelievers amongst them, they would join each other. And if the people were gathered on one plain, all of them unbelievers, except for two believers amongst them, they would join each other."

Ibn Baṭṭah, Al-ʾIbānah Al-Kubrā 1:455

It is reported that ʿAlī said:

"When you learn knowledge, preserve it, and do not mix it with laughter and falsehood, such that the hearts refuse (dislike) it."

Al-Khaṭīb Al-Baghdādī, Al-Jāmiʿ li-Akhlāq Al-Rāwī wa Ādāb Al-Sāmiʿ 1:232

It is reported that ʿAbdullāh bin Masʿūd said:

"It is part of sure belief (yaqīn) [in Allāh] that you do not please the people by angering Allāh, and do not praise anyone [else] for what Allāh has provided you, and do not blame anyone for what Allāh has not given you. For verily, the provision of Allāh is not gained by the keenness of those who are keen [for you to have it], nor is it prevented by the hatred of those who hate [for you to have it]. And verily Allāh, in His justice, made happiness and joy in being certain and content [with Allāh], and made worry and sadness in doubt and anger."

Hannād bin Al-Sarī, Al-Zuhd, article 535.

It is reported that ʿAbdullāh bin ʿAmr bin Al-ʿĀs said:

"Leave alone what you have nothing to do with, and do not speak about what does not concern you, and secure your tongue like you secure your money."

Ibn Ḥibbān Al-Bustī, Rawḍatu Al-'Uqalā' 1:55.

It is reported that Mālik bin Dīnār said:

"It is better for a man to leave one ḥarām dirham than to give one hundred thousand in charity."

Abū Bakr Al-Daynūrī, Al-Mujālasah wa Jawāhir Al-'Ilm 5:125.

It is reported that Abū Al-Dardā' said:

"There is no good in this life except for one of two men: a man listening carefully, receiving and holding [knowledge]; or someone knowledgeable speaking."

Ibn Ḥibbān, Rawḍatu Al-'Uqalā' 1:42.

It is reported that Abūl-'Āliyah said:

"There will come upon the people a time when their hearts will be derelict of the Qurān; they will find neither sweetness nor pleasure by it. If they fall short of doing what they have been commanded to do, they will say: Allāh is most forgiving, merciful (He will forgive us), and if they do what they have been forbidden from doing, they will say: we will be forgiven, we haven't committed any shirk with Allāh. Their affairs will all be based on [false] hope, having no truth and sincerity with it. They will wear the skins of lambs over hearts of wolves. The best of them in his religion will be someone who compromises."

Imām Aḥmad, Al-Zuhd article 1741.

It is reported that Al-Khalīl bin Aḥmad said:

"Men are of four types: There is the man who knows and he knows that he knows. He is knowledgeable, so follow him and ask him. And there is the man who does not know, and he knows that he does not know. He is ignorant, so teach him. And there is the man who knows, but he does not know that he knows. He is heedless, so remind him. And then there is the man who does not know, but he does not know that he does not know (he thinks he knows). This is the fool (idiot), so beware of him."

Ibn ˤAbd Al-Barr, Jāmiˤ Bayān Al-ˤilm wa Faḍlihī article 1538.

It is reported that Jubayr bin Nufayr said:

"I entered upon Abū Al-Dardā' at his home in Ḥims and found him standing in prayer at his place of prayer. When he sat for tashahhud he started to seek protection with Allāh from al-nifāq (hypocrisy). So when he had finished praying, I said "May Allāh forgive you o Abū Al-Dardā', what have you got to do with nifāq?" He said, "O Allāh forgive!", three times, and replied, "Who can feel secure from trial, who can feel secure from trial? By Allāh, a man can be tested with fitnah in a single hour and turn away from his religion.""

Al-Bayhaqī, Shuʿab Al-Īmān 1:857.

It is reported that Harim bin Ḥayyān said:

"Beware of the sinful scholar (al-ʿālim al-fāsiq)." This reached ʿUmar, so he wrote to him in fear, "Who is the sinful scholar?" He wrote back, "I did not intend but good; this is when there is an imām (leader, taken as an example) who speaks knowledge, but practices sins, confusing the people, and thus they go astray."

Al-Dhahabī, Siyar ʾAʿlām Al-Nubalāʾ 4:49.

Al-Khallāl records that Imām Aḥmad said about the Khawārij:

"Do not sell food or clothes to them, and do not buy from them. And he said, The Khawārij are renegades, an evil people."

Al-Khallāl, Al-Sunnah 1:155

It is reported that ʿUthmān bin ʿAffān once addressed the people in a sermon. He praised Allāh, then said:

"O people! Fear Allāh and obey Him, for piety is a valuable prize. Verily the most intelligent person is he who takes account of himself and works for what comes after death, and acquires through the light (guidance) of Allāh a light for the darkness of the grave. The servant of Allāh should fear lest Allāh the Mighty and Sublime resurrects him blind though he used to see. A few comprehensive words can be enough for a wise man, whereas the deaf (who does not listen to guidance) is being called from afar. And know that whoever Allāh the Mighty and Sublime is with has nothing to fear; but whoever Allāh the Mighty and Sublime is against, then in whom can he hope after Allāh?!"

Abū Bakr Al-Daynūrī, Al-Mujālasah wa Jawāhir Al-ʿIlm 4:116,117.

It is reported that Imām Mālik said:

"Whatever you fool around with, don't fool around with your dīn (religion)."

Al-Lālakāʾī, Sharḥ ʾUṣūl ʾIʿtiqād Ahl Al-Sunnah 1:163

It is reported that Al-Fuḍayl bin ʿAyyāḍ said:

"It has reached me that the scholars of old would practice what they learned when they learned it, and through practicing they would become occupied, and because of being occupied, they would be missed, and when they were missed they were sought after, and when they were sought after they would flee."

Al-Dhahabi, Siyar ʾAʿlām Al-Nubalāʾ 8:439,440

It is reported that it was said to Saʿd bin Abī Waqqāṣ during the time of fitnah:

"Will you not fight? For you are one of the people of shūrā (to be consulted in these affairs), and you are more deserving of this matter (leadership) than others? So he replied: I will not fight until you bring me a sword with two eyes and lips that recognizes the believer from the unbeliever, for I have done jihād and I know jihād."

Abū Nuʿaym, Ḥilyatu Al-Awliyāʾ 1:94

It is reported that ʿAbdullāh bin Masʿūd said:

"There is no comfort or rest for the believer until he meets Allāh."

Wakīʿ bin Al-Jarrāḥ, Al-Zuhd #86

It is reported that a man saw Ibn ʿAbbās holding the tip of his tongue saying:

Woe to you, say what is good and you will reap gain, and be silent from speaking evil and you will be safe.

The man asked him:

O Ibn ʿAbbās, what is the matter that I see you holding the tip of your tongue saying such-and-such?

He replied:

It has reached me that the servant of Allāh will not be as angry at anything on the Day of Resurrection as he will be at his tongue.

Imām Aḥmad, Al-Zuhd p236

Saʿīd bin Jubayr said:

"Tawakkul (reliance and trust in Allah) comprehends all of Īmān."

Hunād bin Al-Sarī, Al-Zuhd #534.

It is reported that ʿAbdullāh bin ʿUmar said:

"Whoever tries to make people hear of his deeds, Allāh will make [some] of His creation hear of him (expose him), and belittle him. Ibn ʿUmar then began to cry."

Wakīʿ bin Al-Jarrāḥ, Al-Zuhd #308.

ʿAbd Al-Raḥmān bin Yazīd reports:

"Al-Rabīʿ bin Khuthaym used to come to ʿAlqamah on the day of Jumuʿah and they would talk. They would call for me and I would come and talk with them. One day, they sent for me and I came. ʿAlqamah said to me, Have you not heard what Al-Rabīʿ bin Khuthaym has come to us with? I replied, And what is that? He said, [Rabīʿ] said a man from the People of Scripture once said to us, Do you not see how much people supplicate but how seldom their prayers are answered? That is because Allāh does not accept except what is sincere and purely for Him. I said, Well ʿAbdullāh [bin Masʿūd] already said the same. He asked, What did he say? I replied, Haven't you heard him say, By Him other

than whom there is none worthy of worship, Allāh does not accept [the deed] of one who seeks to be heard of, or seen, and nor someone who is playing around, [He only accepts the supplication] of one who calls upon Him from the bottom of his heart. He replied, Indeed, [I have heard him say that]."

Hunād bin Al-Sarī, Al-Zuhd #874.

Aḥmad bin Yūnus reports:

"I saw Zuhayr bin Muʿāwiyah come to Zāʾidah bin Qudāmah and speak to him to get him to narrate ḥadīth to a man, so Zāʾidah asked, Is he from Ahl Al-Sunnah? Zuhayr replied, I do not know that he has any bidʿah. Zāʾidah said, No, that is another matter! Is he from Ahl Al-Sunnah? Zuhayr said, Since when have people become like this? Zāʾidah replied, Since when did people curse Abū Bakr and ʿUmar?!"

Al-Khaṭīb Al-Baghdādī, Al-Jāmiʿ li Akhlāq Al-Rāwī #754.

It is reported that Ḥudhayfah said:

"How will you be (in the end times) when you open up your religion like the woman who opens her legs to expose her qubul not stopping anyone from coming to her?"

Abū ʿAmr Al-Dānī, Al-Sunan Al-Wāridah fī Al-Fitan #241

It is reported that Al-Ḥasan Al-Baṣrī said:

"Verily, you will find the believer (muʾmin) consistent time after time, upon one way, showing the same face; [whereas] you will find the hypocrite (munāfiq) changing colors, trying to be like everyone around him, running with every wind."

Abū Bakr Al-Daynūrī, Al-Mujālasah wa Jawāhir Al-ʿIlm #1936

It is reported that Imām Al-Zuhrī said:

"We used to sometimes come to a scholar and what we learned of his manners was more beloved to us than the knowledge we took from him."

Abū Nuʿaym, Ḥilyatu Al-ʾAwliyāʾ #4575

It is reported that a man once wrote to Ibn ʿUmar:

"Please write down all knowledge for me. Ibn ʿUmar replied: Knowledge is vast, but if you can meet Allāh having kept your back light of the burden of people's blood, your stomach void of people's wealth and having kept your tongue from [disparaging] their honour, then do so."

Al-Dhahabī, Siyar ʾAʿlām Al-Nubalāʾ 3:222

It is reported that Al-Fuḍayl bin ʿAyyāḍ said:

"Do not mix except with those who have good character; for the one who has good character brings nothing but good, whilst the one who has bad character brings nothing but evil."

Al-Bayhaqī, Shuʿab Al-Īmān, #87044

It is reported that Abū Muslim Al-Khawlānī said:

"The example of the scholars on earth is that of the stars in the sky: when they appear, the people are guided (they navigate using the stars), but when they disappear, the people get confused and lost."

Al-Bayhaqī, Al-Madkhal ilā Al-Sunan Al-Kubrā #287

It is reported that Imām Al-Shāfʿee said:

"The loftiest in status are those who do not know their own status, and the most virtuous of them are those who do not know their own virtue."

Al-Dhahabī, Siyar ʾAʿlām Al-Nubalāʾ 10:99

It is reported from Al-Shaʿbī that he said:

"ʿAbdul-Malik [ibn Marwān, the Khalīfah] once sent me to the king of the Romans, and I stayed with him for a number of days. When I wanted to leave, he asked me, Are you from the House of [your] king (his family)? I replied, I am just a man from the Arabs. He gave me a parchment and said, Deliver this to your companion (the Caliph). When ʿAbdul-Malik had read it, he said to me, Do you know what it says? I replied, No. He said, It says in it, I wonder at a people who have made other than this man king over them. I said, By Allāh, if I had known I would not have carried it to you. [The Roman king] only said this because he has not seen you. ʿAbdul-Malik said, Rather, he envied me for having you, and was trying to incite me to kill you. This reached the Roman king; and when it did, he said, I wanted nothing but this."

Ibn Al-ʿImād, Shadharāt Al-Dhahab 2:26

It is reported that a man came to ʿAlī and asked, *What do you think about a man who committed a sin?* He replied, *He must seek Allāh's forgiveness and repent to Him.* [The man] said, *He did that, but then sinned again?* [ʿAlī] said, *He must seek Allāh's forgiveness and repent to Him. The man again said, He did that, but returned to sin. [*ʿAlī] said, *He must seek Allāh's forgiveness and repent to Him.* The man said for the fourth time, *He did, but then sinned again.* ʿAlī then said, *Until when?* Then he said, *He* *must seek Allāh's forgiveness and repent to Him; and not give up until it is Shayṭān who is defeated [overcome].*

Hunād bin Al-Sarī, Kitāb Al-Zuhd article 910

It is reported that a shaykh (older man) once came and greeted 'Alī, wearing a cloak decorated with silk at the front. He said to the man, *What is this filth under your beard*? The man looked around and said, *I do not see anything*. Another man said, *He means the silk embroidery*. The shaykh said, *In that case, we will throw it away and never wear [such a thing] again.*

Ibn Abī Shaybah, Al-Muṣannaf article 25187

It is reported that Hasan bin Rabī' asked 'Abdullāh bin Al-Mubārak about the meaning of the hadith, "Seeking knowledge is obligatory upon every Muslim". He replied:

It is not [the expert knowledge of hadith and fiqh] you are seeking. Seeking knowledge is an obligation when a man comes to something concerning his religion (dīn): he is to ask about it until he knows it.

Al-Khatīb Al-Baghdādī, Al-Faqīh wa Al-Mutafaqqih article 162.

It is reported that Ibrāhīm bin Ad-ham said:

"Delving into falsehood removes the ability to recognize the truth from the heart."

Abu Nu'aym, Hilyatu Al-Awliyā` 8:22.

It is reported that Wahb bin Munabbih used to say:

"The believer mixes with others in order to learn, keeps quiet to keep safe (from sinning), speaks in order to understand, and secludes himself for the attainment (of good)."

Ibn Abī Al-Dunyā, Al-'Uzlah article 99.

It is reported that Abū Hurayrah said:

"Three things are from Imān: when a man has nocturnal emission during a cold night, so he gets up – only Allāh sees him – and he has a full wash (ghusl); when a person fasts on a hot day; and when a man prays in a barren land, where none but Allāh sees him."

Al-Bayhaqī, Shu'ab Al-Īmān article 51

It is reported that Ya'lā bin 'Ubayd said, "We entered upon Ibn Sūqah, who said: 'O nephew, let me relate to you something that will hopefully benefit you; for it benefited me. 'Atā bin Abī Rabāh once said to us:'"

"Those before you used to consider idle talk to be anything other than the Book of Allāh, or the enjoining of good, or the forbidding of evil, or speaking for the sake of your basic living needs. Do you deny that there are recording angels appointed over you? Sitting on your right and your left? Never is a word said except there is an observer prepared to record? Are you not afraid (ashamed) that your record of words and deeds be spread open only to discover that there is nothing of the hereafter in it?"

Al-Dhahabī, Siyar A'lām Al-Nubalā` 5:86

It is reported that Yūnus bin 'Ubayd said:

"I do not know anything rarer than a good dirham (money earnt lawfully) whose owner spends it on something right, or a brother in Islām in whose company one finds peace. And they are only getting rarer."

Abu Nu'aym, Hilyatu Al-Awliyā` 3:17

It is reported that 'Adī bin Hātim said:

"You will remain in a good state as long as you do not approve what you used to know to be wrong or censure what you used to know to be right, and as long as the knowledgeable (scholar) amongst you can speak amongst you without fear."

Ibn Battah, Al-Ibānah Al-Kubrā article 26.

Sa'īd bin Jubayr reports that a man asked Ibn 'Abbās:

"How many kabā`ir (major, deadly sins) are there? Seven?" He replied, "They are closer to seven hundred than seven; except a major sin does not remain so if one (truly) seeks forgiveness [from Allāh], and a lesser sin does not remain so if one insists on continuously doing it (i.e. it becomes a major sin)."

Al-Tabarī, Al-Tafsīr article 9207.

It is reported that Al-Hasan Al-Basrī said:

"Verily, Allāh lets [a person] enjoy a blessing for as long as He wills. But when He is no longer thanked for it, He turns it into a punishment."

Ibn Abī Al-Dunyā, Kitāb Al-Shukr article 17

It is reported that Isḥāq bin Rāhuway said:

"If you ask the ignorant: 'Who are Al-Sawād Al-A'ẓam (Main Body of the Muslims)?' they will say, 'All the people (together).' But they do not know that The Jamā'ah (Main Body) is a scholar who follows the footsteps of the Prophet and his way. So whoever is with him and follows him is [one of] The Jamā'ah, but whoever contradicts him in it leaves The Jamā'ah."

Abū Nu'aym, Ḥilyatu Al-Awliyā` 9:238,239 et al

It is reported that Imām Al-Zuhrī said:

"Those of our scholars who went before us used to say,"Adherence to the Sunnah is salvation, but knowledge is taken away quickly, so the revival of knowledge means the stability of religion and worldly affairs, and the loss of knowledge means the loss of all that.""

Al-Lālakā`ī, Sharh Usūl I'tiqād Ahl Al-Sunnah article 136

'Umar bin Al-Khattāb once entered upon Abū Bakr and found him pulling at his tongue. He said, "*Oh, what are you doing?*" Abū Bakr replied, "*It is this (i.e my speech) that has brought me so much trouble.*"

Mālik, Al-Muatta 2:988

It is reported that Al-Fudayl bin 'Ayyād said:
"*Whoever sees a wrongdoing from his brother and then laughs in front of him has betrayed him.*"

Abū Bakr Al-Daynūrī, Al-Mujālasah wa Jawāhir Al-'Ilm 5:115

It is reported that Mu'āwiyah bin Qurrah said:
"*Those who will be taken to account most on the Day of Resurrection are those who were healthy and unoccupied.*"

Abū Bakr Al-Daynūrī, Al-Mujālasah wa Jawāhir Al-'Ilm 4:152

It is reported that Sufyān bin 'Uyainah said:
"Verily, the Messenger of Allāh is the highest standard; things are measured by him: his character, lifestyle and behavior. Whatever agrees with [these] is true and correct, and whatever contradicts [them] is wrong."

Al-Khaṯīb Al-Baghdādī, Akhlāq Al-Rāwī wa Ādāb Al-Sāmi' article 8.

It is reported that Muḫammad bin Sīrīn said:

"If the Dajjāl appears, I believe the heretics (People of Desires, Bid'ah) will follow him."

Al-Lālakā`ī, Sharḫ Usūl I'tiqād Ahl Al-Sunnah 1:131

It is reported that 'Umar bin Al-Khaṯṯāb said:
"Do not be impressed by the twitter of an individual. But one who fulfils his duty and trust, and refrains from [transgressing] the honor of people is the real man."

Al-Bayhaqī, Al-Sunan Al-Kubrā article 12345.

It is reported that Sufyān Al-Thawrī said:

"There is nothing that corrupts a person or rectifies him more than [his] companion."

Ibn Baṯṯah, Al-Ibānah Al-Kubrā article 504.

Al-Rabī' bin Sulaymān reports:

"Al-Shāfi'ī used to divide the night into three parts: he would write (knowledge) for the first third, pray during the second third and sleep during the last third."

It is reported from Ḥusayn Al-Karābīsī that he said:

"I spent the night with Al-Shāfi'ī. He would pray for about a third of the night. I hardly ever saw him recite more than fifty verses (in the prayer), one hundred at most. Whenever he came to a verse about mercy, he would ask Allāh for His Mercy, for himself and for the believers; and whenever he came to a verse about punishment, he would seek Allāh's refuge from it, and ask salvation for himself and for all the believers. So it is as if both hope and fear were brought together for him."

Al-Bayhaqī, Ma'rifatu Al-Sunan articles 362, 365.

Mālik bin Mighwal said:

Al-Sha'bī once said to me, *"When these [people] report to you from Allāh's Messenger – praise and peace of Allāh be upon him, adhere to it; but when they merely opine, throw it in the trash."*

Al-Dārimī, Al-Sunan 1:78.

It is reported that Al-Ah̲naf bin Qays said:

"I find it amazing how anyone who passed through the urinary tract twice could ever be arrogant and haughty!"

Al-Dhahabī, Siyar A'lām Al-Nubalā` 4:92.

It is reported that 'Abdullāh bin Mas'ūd said:

"The people will remain upon goodness as long as knowledge comes to them from the Companions of Allāh's Messenger – Allāh's praise and peace be upon him, and from their seniors. But when knowledge comes to them from their minors, that is when they will be destroyed."

Ibn 'Abd Al-Barr, Jāmi' Bayān Al-'Ilm wa Faḍlihi article 1060.

It is reported that Ibrāhīm bin Ad-ham said:

"Zuhd (abstinence from materialism, asceticism) is of three types: (i) obligatory zuhd, (ii) virtuous zuhd and (iii) zuhd for safety. Obligatory zuhd is to abstain from what is forbidden (ḥarām); virtuous zuhd is to be disinterested in what is allowed (of this world); and zuhd for safety is to stay away from doubtful matters."

Abū Bakr Al-Daynūrī, Al-Mujālasah wa Jawāhir Al-'Ilm article 905.

It is reported that 'Alī bin Abī Ṭālib said:

"Mention what you will of the greatness of Allāh, but Allāh is greater than anything you say. And mention what you will of the Fire, but it is more severe than anything you say. And mention what you will of Paradise, but it is better than anything you say."

Abū Bakr Al-Daynūrī, Al-Mujālasah wa Jawāhir Al-'Ilm article 853.

It is reported that Al-Ḥasan Al-Baṣrī said:

"How strange it is that a people whose departure (from this world to the next) has been announced, and whose predecessors have already departed, still play around!"

Abū Bakr Al-Daynūrī, Al-Mujālasah wa Jawāhir Al-'Ilm article 843.

It is reported that Muhammad bin Al-Hanafīyah said:
"Whoever has self respect does not give any value to the worldly life (dunyā)."

Ibn Al-Jawzī, <u>S</u>ifatu Al-<u>S</u>afwah 2:77.

It is reported that Al-<u>H</u>asan Al-Ba<u>s</u>rī once said during the funeral of a man:

"May Allāh have mercy on the man who works for the likes of this day; for today you are able to do what these brothers of yours, the residents of these graves, cannot do. So make full use of your health and free time before the day of distress and accounts comes upon you."

Ibn Abī Al-Dunyā, Dhamm Al-Dunyā article 53.

Abū Ja'far reports:

"Whenever Ibn 'Umar heard a ḥadīth from Allāh's Messenger he never went beyond it, and he never fell short of it."

Ibn Mājah, Al-Sunan, ḥadīth #4. Shaykh Al-Albānī graded this narration ṣaḥīḥ in his edition of the Sunan.

Shaykh Al-Albānī explained that 'he never went beyond it' means: he never added anything to what was in the ḥadīth or overstepped the bounds of the ḥadīth; and 'he never fell short of it' means: he never neglected what was in the ḥadīth.

It is reported on the authority of Al-Walīd bin Mazyad that he said:

"I heard Al-Awzā'ī say, when I asked him, "Who is a fool?" He replied, "One who is blind to what is wrong (evil), [though] he has insight into what is good.""

Al-Dhahabī, Siyar A'lām Al-Nubalā` 7:116.

It is reported that Masrūq said:
"To (be guaranteed) one day in which I issue correct and just verdicts (fatwā) is more beloved to me than fighting in battle (ghazwah, jihād) for a year."

Al-Dhahabī, Siyar A'lām Al-Nubalā` 4:66.

It is reported that Yūnus bin 'Ubayd (d. 139H) said:

"I only liken the worldly life (dunyā) to a man who, whilst sleeping, sees in his dream things he likes and things he does not like. Then he wakes up (the world ends and the next life starts)."

Ibn Abī Al-Dunyā, Dham Al-Dunyā article 21.

It is reported that Al-Ḥasan Al-Baṣrī said:

"The dunyā, from its beginning to its end, is only like a man who takes a nap, sees in his dream what pleases him, and then wakes up."

Abū Bakr Al-Daynūrī, Al-Mujālasah wa Jawāhir Al-'Ilm article 2056.

It is reported that Harim bin Ḥayyān said:

"Never does the servant turn wholeheartedly to Allāh except that Allāh turns the hearts of the believers to him, providing him their love."

Al-Dhahabī, Siyar A'lām Al-Nubalā` 4:49.

Harim bin Ḥayyān was one of the Successors, deputized by 'Umar, and known for his devoutness.

Mu<u>h</u>ammad Ibn Al-<u>H</u>anafīyah said:

"He is not wise who does not live in a good way with the person he has no choice but to live with, until Allāh gives him relief from that [situation]."

Al-Dhahabī, Siyar A'lām Al-Nubalā` 4:117

Imām Al-Zuhrī said:

"Verily, knowledge has calamities [that afflict it]. One of its calamities is when the scholar is left, until he goes away with his knowledge. Another calamity is forgetting [knowledge]. Yet another calamity is lying about [knowledge], and this is the worst type."

Ibn 'Abd Al-Barr, Jāmi' Bayān Al-'Ilm article 684.

It is reported that Ibrāhīm Al-Taymī said:

"What a great difference there is between you and those people [the Salaf]! Worldly wealth came to them but they fled from it, whereas the world turns its back on you and you go after it."

Ibn Al-Mubārak, Al-Zuhd wa Al-Raqā`iq article 538.

It is reported that Al-Hasan Al-Basrī said:

"By Allāh, never was a person given an abundance of worldy wealth and then not feared this might be a plot against him [for his wrongdoing] except a person lacking intelligence and sound opinion. And never has Allāh held back worldy wealth from a person and that person has not thought that a good choice has been made for him except a person who [also] lacks intelligence and sound opinion."

Ibn Abī Al-Dunyā, Dham Al-Dunyā article 42.

It is reported that 'Imrān bin Husayn was once relating hadīth amongst a group of people, when a man said:

"Leave this and give us something from the Book of Allāh. 'Imrān said, "You are a dunce (stupid). Do you find in the Book of Allāh details of prayer. Do you find in the Book of Allāh details of fasting!? This Qur`ān prescribes those matters, and the Sunnah explains them.""

Al-Harawī, Dham Al-Kalām article 244, et al with various wordings.

It is reported that 'Abdullāh bin Aḥmad bin Ḥanbal said: *"I asked my father, "Who are the [real] people?" He replied, "The [real] people are none but those who say ḥaddathanā and akhbaranā (those who report ḥadīth).""*

Abū Bakr Al-Daynūrī, Al-Mujālasah wa Jawāhir Al-'Ilm article 3438.

It is reported that Abū 'Ubaydah bin Al-Jarrāḥ said:
"O people! Yes, I am a man from Quraysh, but there is not a white man (literally: red), nor a black man amongst you who exceeds me in righteousness (taqwā) except that I wish I was in his skin."

Al-Dhahabī, Siyar A'lām Al-Nubalā` 1:18.

It is reported that Mufaddal bin Muhalhal said:
"If the heretic started mentioning his bid'ah right at the beginning of the sitting, you would be on your guard and flee from him, but what he does is begin by mentioning ḥadīth from the Sunnah. Then, he slips his bid'ah in on you. It might then stick to your heart; but when will it leave your heart?"

Ibn Battah, Al-Ibānah Al-Kubrā, 2:444.

Imām Sa'īd bin Al-Musayyib once saw a man praying more than two rak'ah after the beginning of Fajr, making many bows and prostrations, and so he forbade him. The man said, "*O Abu Muḥammad, is Allāh going to punish me for praying?*" Sa'īd said, "*No, but He will punish you for contradicting the Sunnah.*"

Al-Bayhaqī, As-Sunan Al-Kubraa 2:466. graded ṣaḥīḥ by Shaykh Al-Albānī. See Irwā Al-Ghalīl2:236.

It is reported that Khālid bin Ma'dan said:
"*Whoever seeks praise by going against the truth, Allāh will throw it back upon him as blame, and whoever faces blame in order to conform to the truth, Allāh will return it as praise for him.*"

Al-Dhahabī, Siyar A'lām Al-Nubalā` 4:540.

It is reported that Al-A'mash said:
"*They (the Salaf) never used to ask about [the religious condition of] a man after knowing three things about him: where and upon whom he entered, where and with whom he walked, and the close company he kept.*"

Meaning: Knowing these things about a man is more than sufficient for knowing whether he is following the right path on the Sunnah or not.

Ibn Battah, Al-Ibānah article 419.

Ḥudhayfah bin Al-Yamān said:

"*The munāfiqūn (hypocrites) amongst you today are worse than those in the time of Allāh's Messenger.*"

He was asked, "How is that o Abū ʿAbdillāh"?
He replied:
"Because those [in the time of the Prophet] used to hide their nifāq (hypocrisy), whereas the hypocrites of today commit [hypocrisy] openly."

Al-Bukhārī, Al-Ṣaḥīḥ hadith 7113.

It is reported that 'Umar bin Al-Khaṯṯāb came out one Eid. Passing by a group of women, he could smell the scent of perfume from one of them. He asked, *"Who is the one wearing this scent? By Allāh, if I knew who she was, I would do such-and-such (punish her). A woman is only to wear perfume for her husband, and if she goes out, she wears her older (scruffier) clothes or the older clothes of her servant."* And so it was rumoured amongst the women that the woman [who was wearing perfume in public] got up from that gathering having soiled herself (out of fear).

Ibn Abī Shaybah, Al-Muṣannaf article 6387.

It is reported that 'Abdullāh bin Masʿūd said:

"This world (the dunyā) is [only taken as] a home by those who will have no real home [in Jannah], and it is the wealth of those who will have no real wealth, and it is gathered and collected for by those who have no real intelligence."

Ibn Abī Al-Dunyā, Dhamm Al-Dunyā article 16.

It is reported that Al-Ḥasan Al-Baṣrī said:

"To learn a single topic of knowledge and teach it to a Muslim is more beloved to me than having the whole world and giving it in the cause of Allāh."

Al-Khaṭīb Al-Baghdādī, Al-Faqīh wa Al-Mutafaqqih article 53.

It is reported that 'Abdullāh bin Masʿūd said:

"By Allāh, he who gives people verdicts (fatwā) for every question they ask him is crazy (majnūn)."

Ibn Ba<u>tt</u>ah Al-'Ukbarī, Ibṭāl Al-Ḥiyal article 81.

It is reported that Abū Qilābah said:

"It is only the storyteller-preachers (al-quṣāṣ) who have killed knowledge. A man listens to a storyteller for a year without really learning anything that will last, whereas a man who sits with a scholar for an hour learns what will last and benefit him before he even gets up."

Abō Nu'aym, Ḥilyatu Al-Awliyā` 2:287.

It is reported that Imām Aḥmad bin Ḥanbal said:

Al-Shāfi'ī saw me sitting in his circle, and there was some ink on my shirt I was trying to hide. He said, "*Young man, why are you hiding it? Having ink on ones clothes is a sign of lofty conduct: to the sight it is black, but to the insight it is white (with the light of knowledge).*"

It is reported that 'Abdullāh bin Al-Mubārak said:

"Ink on the clothes is the perfume of the scholars."

It is reported that Imām Aḥmad said, seeing the students of ḥadīth approaching with their ink-pots:

"These are the lanterns of Islām."

Al-Khaṭīb Al-Baghdādī, Al-Jāmi' li-Akhlāq Al-Rāwī, articles 508, 509, 512 .

'Alī bin Abī Khālid reports:

I once said to Aḥmad, "This shaykh – referring to an older man who was with us – is my neighbor. I told him not to keep the company of a certain person, and he would like to hear what you have to say about him: I am referring to Ḥārith Al-Qaṣīr (Al-Ḥārith Al-Muḥāsibī). Many years ago, you saw me with him and told me not to sit with him nor speak with him. I have not spoken to him since that time. This shaykh, however, does sit with him. So what do you say?"

I saw Aḥmad go red with anger, his eyes bulging; I had never before seen him like this. He started to say, "Him! May Allāh do such-and-such to him! Only those well-informed of him know what he really is, only those who really know him know what he is. Al-Mughāzilī, Ya'qūb and so-and-so sat with him, and he caused them to adopt the views of Jahm (Ibn Ṣafwān, leader of the Jahmites). They were destroyed because of him."

The old man said, "But Abū 'Abdillāh, he reports ḥadīth, and he is mild and humble; he has done such-and-such [good works]." Abū 'Abdillāh (Imām Aḥmad) became angry and began repeating, "Let not his humility and softness deceive you". He also said, "Do not be fooled by his bowed head, he is an evil man; only those well-informed of him through experience know him. Do not speak to him – with all disrespect to him. Are you going to sit with everyone who narrates from Allāh's Messenger – may the praise and peace of Allāh be upon him – though he be a heretic (mubtadi')? No, with all disrespect."

Ṭabaqāt Al-Ḥanābilah, article 325.

It is reported that Abū Bakr Al-Maṭū'ī said:

"I sat in the circle of Abū 'Abdillāh Aḥmad bin Ḥanbal for twelve years while he read the Musnad to his children, and I never wrote a single ḥadīth, I only looked at his behavior, character and etiquette."

Ibn Al-Jawzī, Manāqib Aḥmad, article 210.

It is reported that Sufyān Al-Thawrī said:

"A man who wanted to write ḥadīth would [learn] manners and worship for twenty years before starting."

Abū Nu'aym, Ḥilyatu Al-Awliyā`, 6:361.

It is reported that Al-Ḥasan Al-Baṣrī said:

"It has reached me that when Allāh the Mighty and Majestic blesses a people and gives them some good he asks them to be grateful. If they are grateful, He is all-able to give them more. But if they are ungrateful, He is all-able to turn His blessings into a punishment."

Al-Bayhaqī, Shu'ab Al-Imān article 4536.

It is reported that Al-Ḥasan Al-Baṣrī said:

"One who acts without knowledge is like one who travels off the path; and the one who acts without knowledge corrupts more than he rectifies. So seek knowledge in a way that does not harm your worship, and seek to worship [Allāh] in a way that does not harm [your seeking of] knowledge. For verily, there were people (the Khawārij extremists) who sought to worship [Allāh] but

abandoned knowledge until they attacked the Ummah of Muḥammad with their swords. But if they had sought knowledge, it would not have directed them to do what they did."

Quoted by Ibn 'Abd Al-Barr, Jāmi' Bayān Al-'Ilm wa Faḍlihi article 905.

Thābit Al-Bunānī, Qatādah and Ibn 'Aṭīyah all report:

"When Anas bin Mālik used to finish a complete reading of the Qur`ān he would gather his wife and children and supplicate for them."

Al-Firyābī, Faḍā`il Al-Qur`ān article 83; Al-Dārimī, Al-Sunan hadith 3477

Imām Sa'īd bin Al-Musayyib said:

"The Sunnah of Al-Fiṭr consists of three things: Walking to the prayer place (muṣallā), eating before leaving [for the prayer] and taking a full bath."

Al-Firyābī, Aḥkām Al-'Eidayn #18.

It is reported that 'Abdullāh bin Mas'ūd said:

"Allāh the Mighty and Sublime laughs at two men [being pleased with them]: a man who stands in the middle of the night while his family sleeps; he purifies himself and stands in prayer, so Allāh laughs at him. And a man who meets the enemy [in battle] and his comrades are defeated; but he stands his ground until Allāh the Mighty and Sublime gives him martyrdom."

Abū Bakr Al-Ājurrī, Faḍl Qiyām Al-Layl, article 9.

It is reported that the son of Al-Fuḍayl bin 'Ayyāḍ said to his father:

"Father! How sweet (beautiful) the speech of the Companions is! [Al-Fuḍayl] said, "Son, do you know why it was so sweet?" He replied, "No father, I do not." He said, "Because they sought Allāh the Exalted when they spoke.""

Al-Bayhaqī, Shu'ab Al-Īmān 2:299

It is reported that Imām Muḥammad bin Sīrīn said:

"There were people who abandoned knowledge and sitting with the scholars, and [instead] took to their chambers and prayed until their skin dried [from exertion in worship]. Thereafter they began to contradict the Sunnah and thus were destroyed. By Allāh, never does a person act without knowledge, except that he spoils and corrupts more than he fixes and rectifies."

Al-Aṣbahānī, Al-Targhīb wa Al-Tarhīb 3:98

It is reported from Al-'Abbās bin Al-Walīd that 'Uqbah said:

"I was once with Arṭa'ah bin Al-Mundhir when one of the people in the gathering said, "What do you say about a man who sits with the followers of the Sunnah and mixes with them, but when the followers of Bid'ah are mentioned he says, 'Spare us from mentioning them, do not talk about them?'" Arṭa'ah said, "He is one of them, do not let him confuse you about his condition." I felt this was strange, so I went to Al-Awzā'ī – and he used to clarify these matters when they came to him. He said, "Arṭa'ah is right, the matter is as he said; this person forbids talking about [Ahl Al-Bid'ah], so how can [people] be on guard against them if they are not exposed?""

Ibn 'Asākir, Tārīkh Dimishq 8:15.

It is reported that the wife of Imām Sa'īd bin Al-Musayyib said:

We only ever used to speak to our husbands like you address your commanders and leaders: [we would supplicate for them when talking to them] "May Allāh keep you right!", "May Allāh keep you well!"

Abū Nu'aym, Ḥilyatu Al-Awliyā` 5:198.

After the death of his wife Umm Ṣālih, Imām Aḥmad, used to praise her. He once said:

"In the thirty years she was with me, we never had a single word of disagreement."

Al-Khaṭīb Al-Baghdādī, Tārīkh Baghdād 16:626.

It is reported that Imām 'Abdullāh bin Al-Mubārak was asked: "Who are the [best] people?"
He replied, "The scholars."
He was asked, "Who are the [real] kings?"
He replied, "the ascetics."
He was asked, "And who are the dregs [of society]?"
He replied, "Those who use their religion as a means of devouring [wealth]."
He was asked, "Who are the rabble?"
He replied, "Khuzaymah bin Khāzim and his companions."
And he was asked, "And who is the low person?"
He replied, "The one who talks about the rise in prices to his guest."

Abū Bakr Al-Daynūrī, Al-Mujālasah wa Jawāhir Al-'Ilm 2:181.

It is reported that Imām Abū Dāwūd Al-Sijistani said:

"Aḥmad bin Ḥanbal never used to involve himself in the things of this world that people involved themselves in; but when knowledge was mentioned, he would speak."

Ibn Al-Jawzī Ṣifatu Al-Ṣafwah 2:519.

It is reported that Al-Ḥusayn bin Muḥammad said:

"Muḥammad bin Ismā`īl Al-Bukhārī was distinguished with three qualities – in addition to the rest of his praseworthy traits: He never spoke much, he never yearned for what people had. He would never occupy himself with other people's affairs; all his attention was towards knowledge."

Al-Dhahabī, Siyar A'lām Al-Nubalā` 12:449

It is reported that Al-Fuḍayl bin 'Ayyāḍ said:

"The believer speaks little and does alot, whereas the hypocrite (munāfiq) speaks a lot and does little. When the believer speaks, it is with wisdom, when he is silent, it is in deep thought, when he sees, he takes lessons, and when he acts, it is a cure. If this is the way you are, then you are in the constant worship [of your Lord.]"

Abū Nu'aym, Ḥilyatu Al-Awliyā` 8:98.

It is reported that Al-Ḥasan Al-Baṣrī said:

"The believer does the best deeds yet is most fearful [that his deeds will not be accepted]. If he were to spend a mountain of wealth [in charity], he would not feel sure [of the reward] until he sees it. The more righteous and pious he becomes, the more he fears. But the hypocrite (munāfiq) says, 'There are so many

people, I will be forgiven, no problem.' So he does wrong and evil deeds, yet holds foolish wishes about Allāh."

Al-Dhahabī, Siyar A'lām Al-Nubalā` 4:586.

It is reported from Ibn Sīrīn that a man once said to Ibn 'Umar:

"Can we offer you some Jawārish? He inquired, "And what is Jawārish?" The man replied, "It is something that will help you digest your food if you get too full up." Ibn 'Umar said, "I have not eaten my fill for four months – not because I cannot find food, but because I have lived with people who used to eat their fill at times and go hungry at others."

Abū Dāwūd, Al-Zuhd article 325.

It is reported that Al-Hasan Al-Basrī said:

"By He in whose Hand is my soul, I have lived amongst people who never ordered food to be prepared for themselves If [food] was presented to one of them, he would eat, otherwise, he would be silent; and he would not care if it was hot or cold."

Abū Nu'aym, Hilyatu Al-Awliyā` 6:270.

It is reported that Al-Fudayl bin 'Ayyād said:

"Two things harden the heart, too much talking and too much food."

Ibn Hibbān Al-Bustī, Rawdatu Al-'Uqalā` p45, Matba'ah Al-Sunnah Al-Muhammadīyah 1949.

It is reported that Mālik bin Dīnār said:

"It is unfitting for a believer that his belly becomes his greatest concern, or that his desires dominate him."

Ibn Abī Al-Dunyā, Al-Jū' (The Book of Hunger) article 105.

'Umar bin Al-Khaṯṯāb said:

"Verily, the followers of opinion are the enemies of the Sunan (the teachings of Allāh's Messenger as passed down in hadith): they were unable to preserve them and their meanings escaped them, and when asked [questions] they were too embarrassed to say 'We don't know,' so they opposed the Sunan with their opinions."

Ibn Abī Zamanīn, Uṣūl Al-Sunnah article 8; Al-Lālakā`ī, Sharḥ Uṣūl I'tiqād Ahl Al-Sunnaharticle 201 et al.

It is reported that Imām Mālik was asked, "Who is allowed to give religious rulings (fatwā)? He replied:

"Issuing fatwā is not allowed except for a person who knows what the people have differed in. It was said, 'Do you mean the different views of the people of opinions (those who depend more on analogy and speculation)? He replied, "No, [I mean] the different views of the Companions of Muḥammad. And he must also know the textual evidence that abrogates [other rulings] and that which is abrogated [by other texts], both in the Quran and the ḥadīth of Allah's Messenger. Such a person can issue fatāwā."

Ibn 'Abd Al-Barr, Jāmi' Bayān Al-'Ilm wa Faḍlihī article 1529.

It is reported that Salmān Al-Fārsī said:

"I would rather die and be resurrected, die and be resurrected, and again die and be resurrected than to see the private part of a Muslim's body or for a Muslim to see mine."

Imām Aḥmad, Al-Zuhd p192. 1st ed. 1983. Dār Al-Kutub Al-'Ilmīyah. Beirut, Lebanon.

It is reported that 'Abdullāh b, 'Umar said:

"Verily, part of disregarding the trust upon you is to look inside [other people's] apartments and houses."

Ibn Abī Al-Dunyā, Kitāb Al-Wara' article 71.

It is reported that Khālid bin Ma'dān said:

"There is not a person except he has four eyes: two in his head with which he sees the matters of this worldly life, and two in his heart with which he looks to the matters of the hereafter. So if Allāh wants good for his servant, He opens his heart's eyes, and so he perceives what he has been promised in the unseen world. Thus he is saved from the unseen [punishment] through the unseen [reward for the obedient]."

Al-Dhahabī, Siyar A'lām Al-Nubalā` 4: 543

It is reported that Imām Al-Shāfi'ī said:

"If you fear becoming deluded and impressed by your deeds then remember whose pleasure you are seeking, and the joy (Paradise) in which you want to be, and what punishment you fear. Whoever thinks about these things will diminish his deeds."

Al-Dhahabī, Siyar A'lām Al-Nubalā` 10:42.

It is reported that Al-Ḥasan Al-Baṣrī said:

"The intelligent person's tongue is behind his heart: when he wants to speak, he first thinks. If [his words] will be in his favor, he says them, and if they will be against him, he does not speak.

And the ignorant person's heart is behind his tongue: when he merely thinks of saying something, he says it, whether it is for or against him."

Abū Bakr Al-Daynūrī, Al-Mujālasah wa Jawāhir Al-'Ilm article 2049.

It is reported that 'Umar bin Al-Khaṯṯāb said:

"I have considered sending out men to the different regions to check on all those who are well off enough but have not made Hajj, and impose the jizyah (tax imposed on Ahl Al-Kitāb in the Muslim state) on them; they are not Muslims, they are not Muslims."

It is also reported that he said:

"If the people abandoned Hajj, we would fight them for it as we fight them for the prayer and zakāh."

It is also reported that he said:

"Whoever dies, being well off enough but having never done Hajj, let him die as a Jew if he wishes or as a Christian."

It is reported that Al-Aswad bin Hilāl said to a freedman of his called Miqlāṣ:

"If you died and had never made Hajj, I would not pray over you."

It is reported that Sa'īd bin Jubayr said:

"If a neighbor of mine died without ever making Hajj, while being well off enough to do so, I would not pray over him."

It is reported that Mujāhid bin Rūmī said:

I asked Sa'īd bin Jubayr, 'Abd Al-Raḥmān bin Abī Laylā and Ibn Ma'qal ('Abdullah Al-Muzanī) about a man who died, being well off enough, but never having made Hajj. Ibn Abī Laylā said, "*I hope that if his next of kin does Hajj on his behalf...*" Sa'īd bin Jubayr said, "*The Fire, the Fire.*" 'Abdullah bin Ma'qal said, "*He died in a state of disobedience to Allāh.*"

Al-Khallāl, Al-Sunnah 5:43-47, articles 1572-1576.

It is reported that Wahb bin Munabbih said:

A scholar once asked another greater than him in knowledge, "How much should I build?" He replied, "As much as shelters you from the sun and the rain." He asked, "How much food should I eat?" He replied, "More than what keeps you hungry and less than what makes you full." He asked, "How much should I wear?" He replied, "As the Messiah (Jesus) did." He asked, "How much should I laugh?" He replied, "As much as appears on your face but does not make audible your voice." He asked, "How much should I cry?" He replied, "Never tire from crying out of the fear of Allāh." He asked, "How much should I hide my deeds?" He replied, "Until people think you had not done a good deed." He asked, "How much should I make public my deeds?" He replied, "As much as will let the keen follow your example but not have the people talk about you."

Wahb said. "*Everything has two ends and a middle. If you grab one end, the other will slant, but if you take the middle, both ends will balance. Stick to the balanced middle in all affairs.*"

Abū Nu'aym, Ḥilyatu Al-Awliyā` 4:45.

Salmān Al-Fārsī once visited a sick friend. When he entered upon him he said:

"Have glad tidings, for verily Allāh makes the illness of a believer an expiation [for his sins] and a cause of being pleased, whereas the illness of a sinner is like a camel that has been tied by its owners, then released by them: it knows not why it was tied up nor why it was released."

Al-Bukhārī, Al-Adab Al-Mufrad in the Chapter on the Expiation [of sins through] illness. Graded ṣaḥīḥ by Shaykh Al-Albānī in Ṣaḥīḥ Al-Adab Al-Mufrad.

It is reported that 'Abdullāh bin Masʿūd said:

"The example of the believer, the unbeliever and the hypocrite is that of three people who arrived at a valley. One of them descended and passed through to the other side. One of them descended until he reached half way, when the third man on the edge of the valley called to him, "Woe to you, where are you going? You will die. Come back." The man who made it to the other side called to him, "Come and be saved." So [the man in the middle of the valley] kept looking back and forth at the two [on each side of the valley], when a flood came into the valley and drowned him. The man who passed through to the other side is the believer; the one who drowned is the munāfiq (hypocrite) –

مُّذَبْذَبِينَ بَيْنَ ذَٰلِكَ لَآ إِلَىٰ هَٰٓؤُلَآءِ وَلَآ إِلَىٰ هَٰٓؤُلَآءِ ۚ

[The Hypocrites] sway between this and that, neither [fully] with the believers nor with the unbelievers.

Quran 4:143

And the one who remained at the edge of the valley [not able to escape the flood and pass] is the kāfir (unbeliever)."

Ibn Abī Ḥātim, Al-Tafsīr article 6144.

Abul-Ḥārith Aḥmad bin Muḥammad Al-Ṣā`igh, the close and respected friend of Imām Aḥmad, reports:

"I asked Abū 'Abdillāh (Imām Aḥmad) about something that had occurred in Baghdād, and [because of which] some people were considering revolting [against the ruler]. I said, "O Abū 'Abdillāh, what do you say about taking part in the revolt with these people?" He decried it and started saying, "Subḥānallāh! The blood [of the people], the blood [of the people]! I do not believe in this and I do not tell others to do it. For us to suffer our situation in patience is better than the fitnah (tribulation) in which blood is spilt, property is taken, and the prohibited are violated (e.g. the honor of women). Do you not know what happened to the people (in the days of the previous fitnah)?" I said, "And the people today, Abū 'Abdillāh, are they not in fitnah [because of the ruler]?" He replied, "If so, it is a limited fitnah, but if the sword is raised, the fitnah will engulf everything and there will be no way to escape. To suffer patiently this [current difficulty], where Allāh keeps your religion safe for you is better for you." I saw him decry revolting against the leaders, and say, "[Do not spill the people's] blood. I do not believe in this and I do not command it.""

Abū Bakr Al-Khallāl, Al-Sunnah article 89.

It is reported that Al-Aḥnaf bin Qays said:

"Restraint is praiseworthy except in three things." People asked, "And what are they o Abū Baḥr?" He replied, "Make haste to do the righteous deed, hurry to conduct the funeral of your deceased, and marry the girl in your charge to a suitable man [as soon as you find him.]"

Abū Bakr Al-Daynūrī, Al-Mujālasah wa Jawāhir Al-'Ilm 6:307.

It is reported that 'Awn bin 'Abdillāh said:

"Those before you used to give to their worldly affairs what was left over from their pursuit of the hereafter. But today, you give to the matters of the hereafter the left-overs from your pursuit of worldly affairs."

Abū Nu'aym, Ḥilyat Al-Awliyā` 10:242.

It is reported that Imām Al-Awzā'ī said:

"At the time of Fajr, or a while before it, the Salaf would be as if birds were sitting on their heads: (still) concentrating on themselves [and their worship], so much so that even if one of their closest friends came to them after having been parted from them, they would not notice him. They would remain in this state until just before sunrise. Then, they would meet each other and sit in the circles. The first thing they would discuss is the matter of their afterlife and what would become of them in the hereafter. Then they would begin the circles of Quran and Fiqh study."

Ibn 'Asākir, Tārīkh Dimishq 35:184, 185.

يَعْلَمُ خَآئِنَةَ ٱلْأَعْيُنِ وَمَا تُخْفِى ٱلصُّدُورُ

Allah knows the fraud of the eyes, and all that the breasts conceal [Quran, Ghāfir (40):19]

It is reported that 'Abdullāh bin 'Abbās said, explaining this verse:

"A man is with a group of people when a woman passes. He shows them that he has lowered his gaze from looking at her. But when he sees they are not paying attention, he looks at her. If

he fears they will notice, he lowers his gaze, but Allāh has seen in his heart that he wishes he could see her body (private areas)."

Hunād bin Al-Sarī, Al-Zuhd article 1428.

It is reported that Anas bin Mālik said:

"There are two days and two nights the likes of which no one has ever heard of before: the Day on which you will receive the news about Allāh the Exalted: whether you will receive His punishment or His mercy, the Day you will be given your book (of deeds): either in your right hand or your left, that [first] night you will spend alone in your grave, a night like no other you have spent, and that night on the morning of which will be the Day of Resurrection, after which there will be no more night."

Abū Bakr Al-Daynūrī, Al-Mujālasah wa Jawāhir Al-'Ilm article 19.

It is reported that Wuhayb bin Al-Ward said:

"Verily, when Allāh the Exalted wants to honor a servant of His (for his righteousness), He afflicts him with a reduced means of living, illness in his body and a fearful life (all of which expiate his sins). Until death comes upon him, and he still has some sins, death is made hard upon him because of them, causing him to meet Allāh with no sins against him.

And when a person is of little value to Allāh (because of his disobedience), He makes his body healthy, broadens his means of living and makes him feel safe (the rewards for any good deeds he did are exhausted). Until death comes upon him, and he still has some good deeds, the experience of death is lightened for him because of them, and he meets Allāh with nothing."

Abu Bakr Al-Daynūrī, Al-Mujālasah wa Jawahir Al-'Ilm article 2865.

It is reported that Al-Sha'bī said:

"Allāh the Exalted distinguished Abū Bakr Al-Ṣiddīq with four qualities He did not distinguish anyone else with: He called him Al-Ṣiddīq (the true believer), and He never named anyone else Al-Ṣiddīq; [Abū Bakr] was the companion of Allāh's Messenger in the cave, and his companion during the Migration (Al-Hijrah); and Allāh's Messenger told him to lead the prayer in the presence of the rest of the Muslims."

Abu Bakr Al-Daynūrī, Al-Mujālasah wa Jawāhir Al-'Ilm article 2815.

It is reported that on the first night of Ramaḍān, 'Umar would pray Maghrib, then say (to the people):

Sit down. Then he would give a small address: "*Verily the fasting of this month has been made a duty upon you, and standing in night prayer has not been made a duty upon you, but those amongst you who can stand in prayer should do so, for it is from the extra good deeds about which Allāh told us: so whoever cannot stand in prayer, let him sleep on his bed.*

And beware of saying: I will fast if so and so fasts and I will stand in night prayer if so and so stands in prayer. Whoever fasts or stands in night prayer, he must make this for Allāh. And you should know that you are in prayer as long as you are waiting for a prayer.

Minimize any vain or false speech in the houses of Allāh (mosques; he said this two or three times). Let none of you fast a few days before the month (in order to avoid missing the beginning of the month; he said this three times). And do not fast until you see [the crescent of the new month] unless it is overcast. If it is overcast, count [the previous month] as 30 days. Then do not break your fasts until you see the night upon the mountain (i.e. you are sure the sun has set)."

'Abd Al-Razzāq Al-Ṣan'ānī, Al-Muṣannaf article 7748.

Mālik bin Dīnār once said:

"Verily you are in greatly troubled times. Only one with true insight knows the times you live in. Verily you are in a time of [people] boasting and being proud. Their tongues are swollen in their mouths, and they seek worldly gain through the deeds of the hereafter. So be warned against them for yourselves, lest they catch you in their nets. O scholar, you are a scholar yet you devour [wealth] with your knowledge. O scholar, you are a scholar yet you boast with your knowledge. O scholar, you are a scholar yet you seek to amass [wealth] with your knowledge. O scholar, you are a scholar yet you transgress [against others] with your knowledge. If you had truly sought this knowledge for Allāh, it would have been seen on you and in your deeds."

Abū Bakr Al-Ājurrī, Kitāb Al-'Ālim Al-Jāhil article 73 et al.

It is reported that 'Abd Al-Raḥmān bin Abzā said:

"A righteous woman with a man is like a great gold-leafed crown on the head of a king, and a bad woman with a man is like a heavy weight upon an old man."

Ibn Abī Al-Shaybah, Al-Muṣannaf article 17428.

It is reported that 'Umar said:

"Fasting does not mean keeping away from only food and drink, it also means keeping away from lying, falsehood, inanity and swearing [by Allāh without need]."

It is reported that Ibrāhīm Al-Nakha'ī said:

"They used to say: lying breaks the fast."

It is reported that Mujāhid said:

"There are two practices, if a person can keep himself from them, his fast will be secured for him: backbiting and lying."

It is related that Abul-'Āliyah said:

"The fasting person is in a state of worship as long as he does not backbite. [1]

It is reported that Ḥafṣah bint Sīrīn said:

"Fasting is a shield as long as one does not tear it, and tearing it is when you backbite." [2]

It is reported that Anas bin Mālik said:

"If the fasting person backbites, his fast is broken." [3]

[1] Ibn Abī Al-Shaybah, Al-Muṣannaf articles 8975, 8980, 8981 and 8982.

[2] 'Abd Al-Razzāq Al-Ṣan'ānī, Al-Muṣannaf articles 8975.

[3] Hunād bin Al-Saree, Al-Zuhd article 1204.

Abul-Mutawakkil Al-Nājī reports:

When Abū Hurayrah and his companions fasted, they would sit in the mosque and say, "let us purify our fast."

Hunād bin Al-Sarī, Kitāb Al-Zuhd, article 1207

It is reported that Imām Al-Awzā'ī used to say:

"Whoever hides his heresy (bid'ah) from us, his companionship is not hidden from us."

Ibn Ba<u>tt</u>ah, Al-Ibānah Al-Kubrā article 420.

It is reported that Ḥafṣah once said to her father ('Umar, during his Caliphate):

"Allāh has increased the provisions; if only you would eat better food than the food you eat now and wear softer clothes then those you wear now?! He said, "I will argue [against] you with your own self: Was not the condition of Allāh's Messenger such-and-such [when you were his wife]!?" He kept reminding her until she cried. He continued, "I have told you, by Allāh, I will share in their hard living (in this world, referring to The Prophet and Abū Bakr) so that I may partake in their good life (in Paradise).""

Hunād bin Al-Sarī, Al-Zuhd article 687; Imām Aḥmad, Al-Zuhd article 201

Suwayd bin Ghaflah reports that 'Umar bin Al-Kha<u>tt</u>āb once took him by the hand and said:

"O Abū Umayah, by Allāh, I know not if we will meet again after today. Fear and obey Allāh your Lord until the Day of Resurrection, as if you see Him, and obey the ruler (imām) even if he is a cut-nosed Abyssinian slave: if he beats you, be patient; if he robs you, be patient and if he belittles you, be patient. And if he tells you [to do something] to the detriment of your religion

(to sin), say: "I hear and obey, [but] my blood goes before my religion." Never leave the Main Muslim Body (Al-Jamā'ah)."

Ibn Zanjawayh, Kitāb Al-Amwāl article 30; Ibn Abī Zamanīn, Uṣūl Al-Sunnah article 205 with a slight variation in wording. Also recorded in other collections.

'Abdullāh bin Shaqīq Al-'Uqaylī said:

"The Companions of Allāh's Messenger did not consider the leaving of any action to be kufr (unbelief), except the prayer (ṣalāh)."

Al-Tirmidhī, Al-Sunan ḥadīth 2622. Graded ṣaḥīḥ by Al-Albānī in his edition of Sunan Al-Tirmidhī.

Ibn Al-Muhallab reports that he heard Abû Mûsā Al-Ash'arī standing on his minbar (pulpit) saying:

"Whoever Allāh has given some knowledge should teach it. And he must not say anything he has no knowledge of, lest he become one of the pretenders and leave the religion."

Ibn Sa'd, Al-Ṭabaqāt 4:102. Maktabah Al-Khānjī, Cairo.

It is reported that Imām 'Abd Al-Raḥmān bin Mahdī said, following a mention of the Ṣûfīah (Sufis):

"Do not sit with them, nor with the followers of Kalām. Be with the carriers of books, for they are like mines, like those who descend: one brings up a gem and another a nugget of gold."

Ibn Baṯṯah, Al-Ibānah Al-Kubrā article 483.

Imām Al-Awzā'ī said:

"Faith (īmān) is not sound except with [correct] words. Faith and words are not sound except with [good] works. And faith, words and deeds are not sound except with [the correct] intentions in conformance to the Sunnah. Those who went before us of our Salaf did not separate faith from deeds: deeds are a part of faith, and faith is from [ones deeds]. īmān is a word that brings together these aspects of the religions [of Allāh] and is confirmed through [a person's] works.

So whoever believes in word, knows in his heart and confirms [his belief] through his works, then this is the strongest handhold that will never break. And whoever says [words of faith] but does not know [faith] in his heart nor confirms it with his works, it will never be accepted of him and he will be in the hereafter from those who suffer in loss."

Ibn Ba tt ah, Al-Ibānah Al-Kubrā article 1097.

It is reported that 'Abdullāh bin Masʿūd said:

"The house in which the Qur'ān is not recited is like a derelict house that has no one to maintain it."

It is also reported that he said:

"Verily the emptiest of houses are those that are empty of the Book of Allāh."

It is reported that Abū Hurayrah used to say about the house in which the Qur'ān is recited:

"It becomes spacious for its inhabitants, the good of it becomes plentiful, the angels come to it and the devils leave it. And the house in which the Qur'ān is not recited becomes cramped for its inhabitants, has little good in it, and the devils come to it."

Ibn Abī Shaybah, Al-Muṣannaf articles 30645, 30647 and 30650.

It is reported that Abū Hurayrah used to say:

"Whoever does not think that his speech is part of his deeds and that his character is part of his religion will be destroyed without even realizing."

Ibn Abī Al-Dunyā Dham Al-Kadhib wa Ahlī article 94.

It is reported that 'Umar bin Al-Khattab said:

"Whoever exposes himself to suspicion, let him blame only himself for whoever suspects him. He who covers his secret is in a position to choose [to correct himself]. Assume the best about your brother until what comes to you from him overcomes you [and you have to change your opinion]. You can never pay back someone who disobeys Allāh in his dealings with you with anything better than obeying Allāh in your dealings with him. Take righteous brothers [as friends]; acquire them in plenty, for they are a beautification in prosperity and an aid during calamity. Do not ask about what has not yet happened until it actually happens, for what has happened is enough of an occupation to worry about what has not happened. Let not your speech be given freely except to those who want to hear it and will value it. Do not seek help in fulfilling a need you have except from someone who wants success for you in that endeavor. Do not consult except people who fear Allāh, and do not accompany the sinner, [lest] you learn his sinfulness. And be humble at the graves."

Abū Dāwūd, Kitāb Al-Zuhd article 89.

It is reported that 'Umar bin Al-Khaṯṯāb once addressed the people and said:

"No man can have anything better after faith (īmān) than a woman of righteous character, loving and child-bearing. And no man can have anything worse after unbelief (kufr) than a sharp-tongued woman of bad character."

Al-Ḥāfidh Abul-Qāsim Al-Aṣbahānī, Al-Targhīb wa Al-Tarhīb article 1528.

It is reported that Mujāhid said:

"Those who strive and exert themselves (al-mujtahid) amongst you today are like those who used to play around amongst those before you."

Wakī' bin Al-Jarrāh, Al-Zuhd article 221.

It is reported that 'Abdullāh bin Masʿūd said:

"If I had ten days left to live, and I knew I would die by the end of them, and I had enough time to get married, I would get married for fear of temptation (fitnah)."

Sa'īd bin Mansūr, Al-Sunan article 493.

It is reported that 'Alī bin Abī Tālib wrote to Salmām Al-Farsī saying:

"The likeness of this worldly life (dunyā) is that of a snake: soft to the touch, it will kill you with its poison. So turn away from what impresses you of it, since what stays with you is so little. And do not be concerned about it, since you are certain about its parting. And be most happy in it when you are most heedful of it;

for every time its companion takes solace in one of its delights, it gives way to one of its woes."

Ibn Abī Al-Dunyā, Kitāb Al-Zuhd article 164.

It is reported that Al-Hasan Al-Basrī said:

"Four signs of wretchedness are: [having] a hard heart, dry eyes [that never cry], extended hopes [about this life], and greed and keenness to amass worldly things (the dunyā)."

Ibn Abī Al-Dunyā, Kitāb Al-Zuhd article 36.

It is reported that some people asked 'Alī bin Abī Ṭālib to describe this worldly life (the dunyā). He said:

"Do you want a long description or a brief one? They replied, "a brief one." He said, "Its permissible things (ḥalāl) [lead to] accounts being taken from you, and its forbidden things (ḥarām) [lead to the] Fire."

Ibn Abī Al-Dunyā, Dham Al-Dunyā article 17.

It is reported that Sufyān Al-Thawrī said:

"If you loved a man for Allāh and then he innovates in Islām and you don't hate him for it, you never [truly] loved him for Allāh."

Abū Nu'aym, Hilyatu Al-Awliyā` 7:34.

It is reported that Ayyūb Al-Sakhtiyānī said:

"Whoever loves Abū Bakr has upheld the religion, whoever loves 'Umar has made the way clear, whoever loves 'Uthmān is enlightened by the light of Allāh, and whoever loves 'Alī has taken the firmest handhold. Whoever speaks well of the Companions of Allāh's Messenger is clear of hypocrisy (nifāq),

but whoever belittles any one of them or dislikes [any one of them] for something he did, then he is a heretic (mubtadi'), an opponent of the Sunnah and the Righteous Predecessors (the Salaf), and it is feared that none of his deeds will be raised to the heavens until he loves all of [the Companions] and his heart is clear towards them."

Ibn Abī Zamanīn, Uṣūl Al-Sunnah article 189.

Abdullāh bin 'Abbās said:

"O Muslims, how can you ask the People of the Book [about their scripture] when the Book of Allāh that was revealed to your is the most recent news of Allāh; you recite it complete and unaltered? Allāh has informed you that they replaced what Allāh wrote and changed the Book with their hands and said 'This is from Allāh,' to purchase with it a measly price (Quran 2:79). Does not the knowledge that has come to you forbid you from asking them? By Allāh, we have not seen a single man among them asking you about what was revealed to you."

Al-Bukhārī, Al-Ṣaḥīḥ hadith 2685, Chapter on not asking the Polytheists for testimonies or anything else. He also records it in other chapters.

It is reported that Abū Ḥāzim Al-Ashja'ī said:

"If you find yourself in a time when speech is accepted as knowledge and knowledge is accepted as deeds [instead of putting it into practice], then you are in the worst time and with the worst people."

Abū Bakr Al-Daynūrī, Al-Mujālasah wa Jawāhir Al-'Ilm` 4:338.

Abd Al-Raḥmān bin Mahdī reports:

"I entered upon Mālik bin Anas when a man was asking him about the Qur`ān. [Imām Mālik] said, "Perhaps you are a companion of Amr bin 'Ubayd. May Allāh curse 'Amr, for he was the one who innovated this bid'ah of Kalām . If Kalām was knowledge, the Companions and their Followers would have spoken it, like they spoke about the regulations and laws [of Islam]. But [Kalām] is falsehood that leads to falsehood.""

Abul-Faḍl Al-Muqri`Al-Rāzī, Aḥādīth fī Dham Al-Kalām wa Ahlihī p96.
Al-Harawī, Dham Al-Kalām wa Ahlihī no.874.

It is reported that 'Abdullāh bin Al-Mubārak said:

"It is right that an intelligent person does not undervalue three [types of people]: the scholars, the rulers, and [his Muslim] brothers. Whoever undervalues the scholars will lose his afterlife, whoever undervalues the rulers will lose his worldly life, and whoever undervalues his brothers loses his good character and conduct."

Al-Dhahabī, Siyar A'lām Al-Nubalā`17:251.

It is reported that Al-Ḥasan Al-Baṣrī said:

"If people called on Allāh when put to trial because of their rulers, Allāh would relieve their suffering; but instead they resorted to the sword, so they were left to it. And not one day of good did they bring.

Then he recited (Quran 7: 137):
And the good word of your Lord was fulfilled for the Children of Israel, for the patience and perseverance they had, and We

destroyed the works of Pharaoh and his people and what they had erected."

Ibn Abī Ḥātim, Al-Tafsīr no. 8897.

Anas reports that when Salmān [Al-Fārsī] was ill, Sa'd visited him and found him crying, so he asked him:

"O my brother, what makes you cry? Did you not accompany the Messenger of Allāh ? Did you not do such-and-such [good deeds]? He replied, "I am not crying over any one of two things: I am not crying out of love and yearning for this world nor out of dislike for the hereafter, but I am crying because Allāh's Messenger took a covenant from me about something I think I have only transgressed. He made me promise that it is enough for anyone only to have enough [of this world] as would suffice as the provisions of a traveler, but I think I have only gone too far. As for you o Sa'd, fear Allāh when you judge, and when you distribute anything and when you think about doing anything."

Thābit (one of the reporters) said, "And it reached me that [when he died] he left only about twenty dirham of spending he had."

Ibn Mājah, Al-Sunan. Shaykh Al-Albānī graded this narration ṣaḥīḥ. See ṣaḥīḥ wa Ḍaʿīf Sunan Ibn Mājah no. 4104.

It is reported that Abū Al-Dardā said:
"You will never be pious (a person of taqwā) until you become knowledgeable, and you will never be beautiful with your knowledge until you act [by it]."

Ibn ʿAbd Al-Barr, Jāmiʿ Bayān Al-ʿIlm wa Faḍlihī article 1239.

It is reported that 'Umar bin Al-Khaṯṯāb said:

"We were once in a time when we did not think anyone learned the Quran seeking anything but Allāh the Exalted, but now I fear there are men who learn it and intend the people and what they can get from them. So seek Allāh with your recitation and deeds. For verily, we used to know you when Allāh's Messenger was amongst us, when revelation would descend and Allāh would tell us about you. As for today, Allāh's Messenger has passed on, and the revelation has stopped; and I only know you as I say: whoever shows what is good, we love him for it and think good of him, and whoever shows what is evil, we hate him for it and suspect him. Your secret and private matters are between you and your Lord the Mighty and Majestic."

Al-Ājurrī, Akhlāq Ḥamalat Al-Qur`ān article 26.

It is reported that Al-Fuḍayl bin 'Ayyād said:
"How will you be if you reach a time when you will see people who do not distinguish truth from falsehood, believer from unbeliever, trustworthy from treacherous, nor ignorant from knowledgeable, and neither recognize what is right nor censure what is wrong?"

Ibn Battah, Al-Ibānah Al-Kubrā 1:188.

After reporting this narration, Imām Ibn Battah said:

"To Allāh we belong and to Him we will return! We have reached that time, we have heard this and have come to know most of it and witnessed it. If a man to whom Allāh has bestowed sound reasoning looks and thinks carefully and ponders the matter of Islām and its people and treads the rightly guided path as regards to them, it will become clear to him that most people have turned back on their heals, deviated from the correct path,

and turned away from correct proof. Many people have started to like what they used to hate, allow what they used to forbid and recognize what they used to reject. And for sure this is not the [right] character of the Muslims, nor the behaviour of those who have insight into this religion, and neither of those who believe in it and are certain about it."

Abdullāh bin Masʿūd said:

"When a man amongst us learned ten verses [of the Quran], he would not move on [to the next verses] until he had understood their meanings and how to act by them."

Al-Ṭabarī, Al-Tafsīr 1:80. Shaykh Aḥmad Shākir graded its chain of transmission ṣaḥīḥ.

Yaḥyā bin Yaḥyā Al-Naysābūrī reports:

"I was once with Sufyān bin 'Uyainah, when a man came to him and said, "O Abū Muḥammad, I complain to you of so-and-so", meaning his wife, "I am the lowest and most despicable thing to her." [Sufyān] lowered his head for a few moments, then said, "Perhaps you wanted her in order to better your status." The man said, "Indeed, o Abū Muḥammad." Sufyān said, "Whoever goes for glory will be tried with ignominy, whoever goes for wealth will be tried with poverty, but whoever goes for religiousness, Allah will bring together for him glory and wealth with the religion." He then started to narrate to him:

We were four brothers: Muḥammad, 'Umrān, Ibrāhīm and I. Muḥammad was the eldest, 'Umrān was the youngest, and I was in the middle. When Muḥammad wanted to marry, he desired status and married a woman of higher standing, so Allah tried him with ignominy. 'Umrān desired wealth, so he married a richer woman and Allah tried him with poverty: [her family] took everything from him and gave him nothing.

I pondered their situation. Mu'ammar bin Rāshid once came to us so I consulted him on the situation and told him the story of my brothers. He reminded me of the ḥadīth of Yaḥyā bin Ja'dah and the ḥadīth of 'Ā`ishah. The ḥadīth of Yaḥyā bin Ja'dah states that the Prophet said, "A woman is married for four things: her religion, her status (lineage), her wealth or her beauty; so take the religious one and be successful." The ḥadīth of 'Ā`ishah states that the Prophet said, "The most blessed woman is she who is easiest to maintain."

Thus, I chose [to marry a woman of] religion and modest dowry, in accordance with the Sunnah of Allah's Messenger, and Allah gave me status and wealth along with the religion."

Abū Nu'aym, H̲ilyatu Al-Awliyā` 7:289, 290.

Khālid bin 'Umayr Al-'Adawī reports, 'Utbah bin Ghazwān once gave us a sermon. He praised Allāh, then said:

"The life of this world has announced its departure and is quickly turning away, and nothing remains of it save the likes of the last drop of water in a vessel as its possessor tries to catch it. You are moving on to an abode that has no end, so move on with the best [deeds] that you have. For it has been said to us that a rock can be dropped from the edge of Hell and fall for seventy years without reaching the bottom. Yet, by Allāh, it will be filled. Do you not then wonder? And it has been said to us that a single entrance to Paradise is as wide as a journey of forty years, yet there will come a day when it will be crowded. I have seen myself as the seventh of seven [followers of] Allāh's Messenger – Allāh's

peace and blessings be upon him; we had no food save the leaves of trees which put sores round our mouths. I once got a cloak which I tore in half to share with Sa'd bin Mālik: I used half as my waist-wrap and he used the other. And yet today, there is not one of us except he has become a governor over some city – and I seek refuge with Allāh that I consider myself great and important when I am small in front of Allāh. Verily there was never prophet-hood except that it gradually changed until it ended up being a kingship, and verily you will see what the governors after us are like."

Sahīh Muslim no. 7624

It is reported that 'Alī bin Abī Ṭālib said:

"Goodness is not in your wealth and offspring being plentiful; true goodness is when your [good] deeds are plenty and you have great understanding and forbearance, and when you compete to worship your Lord. If you do good you praise Allāh and thank Him, and if you sin you beg Allāh's forgiveness. There is no good in this life except with two types of men: A man who sins but then corrects himself through repentance, and a man who strives and hastens to get [the good] of the hereafter."

Ibn 'Asākir, Al-Tawbah article 13.

It is reported that:

"ʿAbdullāh bin Al-Ḥasan used to often sit with Rabīʿah. One day they were revising and studying various practices from the Sunnah when a man in the gathering said, "[But] this is not what is practiced [by the people]." ʿAbdullah said, "So if the ignorant become so numerous that they become the rulers and judges, will

they then be a proof over the Sunnah?" Rabīʿah said, "I bear witness that these are the words of the sons of the Prophets.""

Al-Khaṭīb Al-Baghdādī, Al-Faqīh wa Al-Mutafaqqiharticle 384.

Imām Al-Buwayṭī reports:

I heard Al-Shāfi'ī say, *"A man does not become complete in this life except when he has four [qualities]: religiousness (al-diyānah), trustworthiness (al-amānah), safeguarding [from sin] (al-ṣiyānah) and sobriety (al-razānah)."*

Al-Bayhaqī, Manāqib Al-Shāfi'ī 2:189.

Ibn Shihāb reports:

'Umar bin 'Abd Al-'Azīz, said, "The Messenger of Allāh and the authorities (leaders of the Muslims, the Caliphs) after him set certain ways and practices. To follow those ways is to believe in Allāh's Book and to complete [ones] obedience of Him, and to be strong upon the religion of Allāh. It is not for anyone to alter those ways or change them for something else, and it is not for anyone to consider the views and opinions of those who contradict them. Whoever follows what [the Prophet and his Caliphs] laid down will be guided, whoever seeks enlightenment through it will be enlightened. But whoever contradicts those ways and follows a way other than the way of the Believers, Allāh the Mighty and Majestic will leave him in the path he has chosen and land him in Jahannam (Hell); and what an evil destination that is.'"

Al-Lālakā`ī, Sharḥ Uṣūl I'tiqād Ahl Al-Sunnah 1:94.

It is reported that Abū Al-Dardā` said:

"Be a scholar or a learner, or a person who loves [the scholars] or a follower [of the scholars], but do not be the fifth. Ḥumayd (one of the reporters) asked Al-Ḥasan (Al-Baṣri, who reported this from Abū Al-Dardā`), "And who is the fifth?" He replied, "A heretic (mubtadi', religious innovator}."

Ibn ʿAbd Al-Barr, Jāmi' Bayān Al-'Ilm 1:142.

It is reported that Ibrāhīm bin Adham once passed through the market of Baṣrah. People gathered around him and asked:

"O Abū Isḥāq, Allāh the Exalted says in his Book. 'Call on me, I will answer your prayers', but we have been calling on Him for a long time and He does not answer our prayers. [Ibrāhīm] replied, "O people of Baṣrah, your hearts have died in respect to ten things: First, you know Allāh but you do not give Him His rights; second, you have read Allāh's Book but you do not act by it; third, you claim to love Allāh's Messenger yet you abandon his Sunnah; fourth, you claim to be enemies to Shayṭān but you conform to [his ways]; fifth, you say you love Paradise yet you do not work for it; sixth, you say you fear The Fire yet you put yourselves closer to it [by sinning]; seventh, you say death is true but you do not prepare for it; eighth, you busy yourselves with the faults of others and disregard your own; ninth, you consume the favors of your Lord but are not grateful for them; and tenth, you bury your dead but take no lesson from them."

Abū Nu'aym, Ḥilyah Al-Awliyā' 8: 15, 16.

Khawāt bin Jubayr said:

"Sleeping in the first part of the day is ignorance, and in the middle of the day [good] character, and in the last part of the day stupidity."

Al-Bukhārī, Al-Adab Al-Mufrad. Shaykh Al-Albānī graded its chain of transmission ṣaḥīḥ. See Ṣaḥīḥ Al-Adab Al-Mufrad hadith #947.

Abū Bakr Al-Ṣiddīq said:

"I will not leave anything Allāh's Messenger did, except that I will also do it; for I fear that if I were to leave any of his commands and ways I would deviate."

Al-Bukhārī, Al-Ṣaḥīḥ 2:386 ḥadīth no. 3093; Ibn Baṯṯah, Al-Ibānah article 77, and others.

After recording this narration, Ibn Baṯṯah states:

"This, my brothers, is the greatest Ṣiddīq (true believer), fearing that he would fall into deviation if he were to leave any of the commandments of his Prophet. What then is to happen in a time in which people deride their Prophet and his commandments, and compete with each other and show off in contradicting him and mock his Sunnah? We ask Allāh to protect us from slipping and to save us from evil deeds."

It is reported that Al-Fuḍayl bin ʿAyyāḍ said:

"Verily, Allāh has angels who seek out the circles of remembrance [of Allāh], so be careful who you sit with; make sure it is not with an adherent of bid'ah, for Allāh does not look at them. And the sign of nifāq (hypocrisy in faith) is that a man mingles with an adherent of bid'ah."

Ibn Baṯṯah, Al-Ibānah Al-Kubrā 1:460

Abū Al-Dardā` once wrote to Salmān Al-Fārsī:

"Come to the Holy Land. [Salmān] wrote back, "Verily, the land does not make anyone holy; it is the deeds of a man that make him pure.""

Al-Dhahabī, SIyar A'lām Al-Nubalā 1:549.

It is narrated that 'Uthmān bin 'Affān said in a sermon:

"Son of Adam! Know that the angel of death who has been assigned to you has not ceased to pass you and move on to others, ever since you have been in this world. But it is as if he is about to pass someone else and move on to target you, so be careful and prepare for him (by correcting your deeds). And do not forget him, for he does not forget you. And know o son of Adam, if you are heedless about yourself and do not prepare, no one else will prepare for you. You must meet Allah the Mighty and Majestic, so take for yourself and do not leave it to someone else. Peace be on you."

Abū Bakr Al-Daynūrī, Al-Mujālasah wa Jawāhir Al-'Ilm 2: 73, 74.

It is reported that Bishr bin Al-Ḥārith said:

"I heard Al-Fuḍayl bin 'Ayyāḍ say, "It has reached me that Allāh has barred repentance from every adherent of bid'ah (religious innovation), and the worst of the people of bid'ah are those who hate the Companions of Allāh's Messenger." He then turned to me and said, "Make the firmest of your deeds with Allāh your love for the Companions of His Prophet, for [then], were you to come to the standing of judgment (on the Day of Resurrection) with the likes of the Earth in sins, Allāh would forgive you; but if you come [on that Day] with even the smallest amount of hatred for them, no [good] deed will benefit you.""

Abū Bakr Al-Daynūrī, Al-Mujālasah wa Jawāhir Al-'Ilm 5. 412.

It is reported that Abū Al-'Āliyah said:

"I would travel for days to a man to hear [knowledge/ḥadīth] from him, and the first thing I would check about him is his prayer: if he performed it properly I would stay and hear [knowledge] from him, but if he neglected it, I would return without hearing from him, and I would say, 'He will be even more neglectful of other matters.'"

Al-Khaṭīb Al-Baghdādī, Al-Riḥlah fī Ṭalab Al-Ḥadīth article 22; Al-Dhahabī, Siyar A'lām Al-Nubalā` 4:209.

It is reported that Imām Al-Shāfi'ī said:

"When I see a man from the Adherents of Ḥadīth, it is as if I have seen the Prophet alive."

Al-Khaṭīb Al-Baghdādī, Sharaf Ashāb Al-Ḥadīth article 85.

Abū Isḥāq [Al-Fazārī] states:

"The enemy was never able to stand up to the Companions of Allāh's Messenger, so when the news of the defeat of the Romans came to Heraclius at Antioch he asked [his people], "Woe to you, tell me about these people who fight you, are they not humans like you?" They replied, "Indeed, they are." He asked, "So are you more in number or them?" They replied, "We outnumber them greatly in all places." He said, "So how is it that you are defeated whenever you meet them [in battle]." A senior and esteemed elder amongst them replied, "Because they stand in prayer at night, fast during the day, fulfill their agreements and promises, enjoin what is right and forbid what is evil, they are fair and just amongst themselves; and because we drink wine, fornicate,

commit sin, break our agreements, steal, oppress and do injustice, enjoin the committing of what angers Allāh and forbid what pleases Allāh the Mighty and Majestic, and we cause evil and corruption in the land." Heraclius said, "You are the one who has told me the truth.""

Abū Bakr Al-Daynūrī, Al-Mujālasah wa Jawāhir Al-'Ilm 4:91.

It is reported that ʿAbdullāh bin ʿUmar was asked:

Did the Companions of Allāh's Messenger used to laugh? He replied, "*Yes, and the īmān (faith) in their hearts was greater than the mountains.*"

ʿAbd Al-Razzāq Al-Ṣan'ānī, Al-Muṣannaf 11:327.

It is reported that 'Amr bin Maymūn said:

The Companions of Allāh's Messenger used to say, "The mosques are the houses of Allāh on Earth, and it is a right from Allāh that He will honor those who visit Him in [His houses]."

Ibn Al-Mubārak, Al-Zuhd wa Al-Raqā`iq 4:159.

It is reported that ʿUmar bin Al-Khaṯṯāb once came out and saw a travelling party; he asked: *Who is this travelling party?* They replied, "*Pilgrims (on Hajj).*" He asked them three times, "*And nothing else has brought you forth?*" They replied, "*Nothing else.*" He said, "*If the travelers [on Hajj] knew who they were coming to, they would feel the delight of having great virtue after forgiveness [from Allāh]. By He in whose hand is ʿUmar's soul, never does [the pilgrim's] camel raise its hoof and place it back down except that Allāh raises [the pilgrim] in rank, forgives one of his sins and writes for him a good deed.*"

ʿAbd Al-Razzāq Al-Ṣan'ānī, Al-Muṣannaf 5: 4, 5.

It is reported that Ayyūb Al-Sakhtiyānī was asked:

"Is knowledge today greater or lesser [in amount]? He replied, "There is more speech today, but there was more knowledge in the past.""

Al-Fasawī, Al-Ma'rifah wa Al-Tārīkh 2:136.

Al-Aḥnaf bin Qays reports that ʿUmar bin Al-Khaṯṯāb said:

"Nothing is permitted for ʿUmar from the wealth of Allāh except two garments: one for winter and one for summer [heat], and what I need to carry me to Hajj and ʿUmrah. And the provisions for my family are that of an [average] man of the Quraysh: neither the richest nor the poorest amongst them. After that, I am just a man from amongst the Muslims."

Abū Bakr Al-Daynūrī, Al-Mujālasah wa Jawāhir Al-ʿIlm 6:78.

It is reported that Al-Aḥnaf bin Qays said:

"Stay away from mentioning women and food in our gatherings, for I hate a man to constantly describe his private parts and his stomach. It is an aspect of higher conduct and religiousness that a man [sometimes] leaves eating food while he desires it."

Abū Bakr Al-Daynūrī, Al-Mujālasah wa Jawāhir Al-ʿIlm 3:44, 45.

It is reported that when Al-Ḥasan Al-Baṣrī was on his deathbed, some of his companions came to him and said:

O Abū Sa'īd, offer us some words you can benefit us with. He replied, "I will equip you with three words, then you must leave me to face what I am facing. Be the farthest of people from those things you have been forbidden, and be the most involved of people in the good you have been commanded to do; and know that the steps you take are two steps: a step in your favor and a step against you, so be careful where you come and where you go."

Abū Nu'yam, Ḥilyah Al-Awliyā` 2:154

It is reported that Imām Al-Awzāʿī wrote:

"O Muslims, fear Allāh and obey Him, and accept the advice of the sincere advisers and the exhortation of the exhorters, and know that this knowledge is religion, so be careful about what you do [in it] and from whom you take [it] and who you follow and who you trust your religion to. For verily, the followers of Bid'ah are all falsifiers and liars, neither are they careful nor do they fear and protect [against wrongdoing], and nor are they to be trusted to not distort what you hear. They say what they know not when criticizing and decrying or when affirming their lies. But Allāh encompasses what they do. So be on guard against them, suspect them, reject them and distance yourselves from them, for this was what your earlier scholars and the righteous latter ones did and instructed others to do. Beware of rising against Allāh and becoming instruments in the destruction of His religion and undoing its handholds by respecting the innovators, for you know what has come down to us about respecting them. And what stronger respect and veneration can there be than taking your religion from them, following them, believing them, being close to them and helping them in alluring those they allure and attracting those they attract of the weak Muslims towards their ideas and the religion they practice? This is

enough to be considered a partnership and contribution to what they do."

Ibn 'Asākir, Tārīkh Dimishq 6:361, 362.

It is reported that Al-Ḥasan Al-Baṣrī said when asked 'what is īmān (faith)?':

"It is perseverance (al-ṣabr) from the things that are forbidden by Allāh the Mighty and Majestic and acceptance. He was asked, "What is perseverance and acceptance?" He replied, "al-ṣabr is to persevere in holding back from what Allāh has forbidden, and [acceptance is] acceptance of what Allāh the Mighty and Majestic has commanded.""

Abū Bakr Al-Daynūrī, Al-Mujālasah wa Jawāhir Al-'Ilm 3:535.

It is reported that Jundub bin 'Abdillāh Al-Bajalī was once asked for advice and instruction. He said:

"I advise you to fear Allāh and obey Him (taqwā) and I advise you to adhere to the Quran, for it is a light in the dark night and a guidance during the day, so implement it no matter how much struggle and poverty you have to face. If a calamity befalls you, put your wealth forward to protect your religion, and if the calamity continues, put forward your wealth and your life to save your religion [but never risk your religion], for the ruined is he whose religion is ruined, and the looted is he whose religion is taken. And know that there is no poverty after Paradise, and no riches after the Fire."

Al-Dhahabī, Siyar A'lām Al-Nubalā` 3:174.

The likeness [of the munāfiq] is as the likeness of one who kindled a fire; then, when it lighted all around him, Allāh took away their light and left them in darkness. So they could not see. They are deaf, dumb and blind, so they return not [to the Right Path]. (Quran 2:17)

Qatādah said:

"This is the likeness Allāh has given of the Hypocrite (munāfiq); he says lā ilāha illallāh and with it marries into the Muslims, inherits from the Muslims, fights alongside the Muslims, and protects his blood and wealth. But when death comes, [the testimony of faith] has no basis in his heart, and no reality in his actions, so the munāfiq is stripped of it at death and left in darkness and blindness wondering therein, just as he was blind about the right of Allāh and obedience to Him in his worldly life and deaf to the truth."

Al-Ṭabarī, Al-Tafsīr.

It is reported that Al-Ḥasan bin Al-Ḥasan bin 'Alī bin Abī Ṭālib said to a person from the Rāfiḍah:

"Love us, but if we disobey Allāh, then hate us; for if Allāh was going to benefit anyone because of his relation to the Messenger of Allāh, without obedience [to Allāh], He would have benefitted the mother and father [of the Prophet]."

Al-Dhahabī, Siyar A'lām Al-Nubalā` 4:486.

Ibn 'Abbās said, *"Address the people once a week, and if you must do so more often, then twice; and if you have to do even more, then three times; and do not make people tired or bored with the Quran. Let me not find you coming to the people to exhort them and tell them stories while they are speaking amongst themselves, thus interrupting their conversation and tiring them. Instead, listen, and when they tell you, address them when they desire to listen to your speech. And beware of making your supplications rhyme, stay away from this, for I found Allāh's Messenger and his Companions doing nothing but [staying away from this]."*

Al-Bukhārī, Al-Ṣaḥīḥ 'What is hated about making supplications rhyme.'

It was said to 'Ā`ishah, *"There are people who faint when they hear the Quran."* She said. *"The Quran is nobler than to have people lose their minds from it. Rather, it [should be] as Allāh the Mighty and Sublime said:*

Those who fear their Lord tremble with fear by it, then their skins and hearts settle to the remembrance of Allah. (Sūrah Al-Zumar: 23)

Abū 'Ubayd Al-Qāsim bin Sallām, Faḍā`il Al-Qur`ān p214.

It is reported that 'Abdullāh bin 'Urwah bin Al-Zubayr said, *"I asked my grandmother Asmā` (bint Abī Bakr), 'How were the Companions of Allāh's Messenger when they heard the Quran?'* She replied, *'their eyes would shed tears and they would tremble (with fear), as Allāh described them (in the Quran).'* I said, *'There are some people here who, when they hear the Quran, fall down unconscious,'* She said, *'I seek refuge with Allāh from the accursed Shayṭān.'"*

Al-Bayhaqī, Shu'ab Al-Īmān 3:417; Ibn Al-Mubārak, Al-Zuhd wa Al-Raqā`iq 3:54 with a slightly variant wording.

It is reported that 'Abd Al-Raḫmān bin Mahdī said:

"If it were not for the fact I hate that Allah is disobeyed, I would have wished that no one remain in this city except that he had spoken ill of me and backbitten me; for what is nicer than a good deed a man finds in his records on the Day of Resurrection without having done a thing or even having known?"

Abū Nu'aym, Hilyatu Al-Awliyā` 4:45.

It is reported that there was a young man who was from the people of knowledge who used to put himself forward, speak and behave haughtily with his knowledge in front of those older than him. This angered Sufyān [Al-Thawrī], he said, *"The Salaf were never like this; they never used to claim leadership, or sit at the head of the gathering until they had sought this knowledge for thirty years, and you act haughty in front of those who are older than you. Get up, I never want to see you even come close to my circle."*

Al-Bayhaqī, Al-Madkhal ilā Al-Sunan Al-Kubrā 2:74.

Sa'īd bin Al-Musayyib reports from his father, *"I was once sitting with 'Umar when a group of people arrived from Al-Shām. 'Umar enquired about them and how they were; he asked, 'Do the people of Al-Shām hasten to break the fast.' He said, 'Yes.' ['Umar] said, 'They will not cease to remain upon good as long as they do this, and do not wait for the stars [to come out] as the people of Irāq do.'"*

'Abd Al-Razzāq Al-Ṣan'ānī, Al-Muṣannaf 4:225.

Sālim bin 'Ubayd reports, *"I used to stay in the house of Abū Bakr. One night, he prayed for as long as Allāh willed him to. He then said [to me], 'Go and see if al-fajr has started,' so I went, returned and said, 'Whiteness has risen in the sky.' So he prayed for as long as Allāh willed, then said [again], 'Go and see if al-fajr has started.' I went out, returned and said, '[The light] is spreading out and becoming reddish,' to which he said, 'Now bring me my drink (i.e. my pre-dawn meal, al-suḥūr).'"*

Al-Dāraquṭnī, Al-Sunan 2:166. Al-Dāraquṭnī grades its chain of transmission ṣaḥīh.

Al-Bukhārī reports 'Umar came to the Black Stone (performing ṭawāf,), kissed it, and said, *"I know that you are a stone, you do not cause benefit or harm; and if it were not that I had seen Allāh's Messenger kiss you, I would never have kissed you."*

Al-Bukhārī, Al-Ṣaḥīḥ, Chapter on what has been said about the Black Stone.

It is reported that once, some good food was served to Anas [Ibn Mālik] , and [the person who served the food] was well off enough to afford good food. As he was eating, he kept a morsel of the food in his mouth for a while, then looked at the people and began to cry. Then he said, *"By Allāh, I have accompanied people who, if they could get hold of this kind of food, would have fasted even more often, and spent less time not fasting. One of them would find only milk mixed with water [as food], which he would drink and then fast on."*

Al-Mu'āfā bin 'Imrān, Kitāb Al-Zuhd article 215.

It is reported that Abū Al-'Āliyah said, *"I learned writing and the Qur`ān without my family noticing, and not a drop of ink was ever seen on my garment."*

Abū Nu'aym, Ḥilyatu Al-Awliyā` Vol. 2 p217.

It is reported that Al-Fuḍayl bin ʿAyyāḍ said, "*Whoever helps an adherent of bid'ah (heretic) has helped in the destruction of Islam.*"

Abū Nu'aym, Ḥilyatu Al-Awliyā` Vol. 1 p398.

It is reported that Abū Isḥāq Al-Hamdānī and Ibrāhīm bin Maysarah said, "*Whoever respects an adherent of bid'ah has helped in the destruction of Islam.*"

Reported from Al-Hamdānī by Al-Ājurrī, Al-Sharī'ah Vol. 5 p260; and from Ibn Maysarah by Al-Lālakā`ī, Sharḥ Usūl I'tiqād Ahl Al-Sunnah Vol. 1 p265.

It is reported ʿUmar bin Al-Khaṯṯāb said, "*Stay well away from the enemies of Allāh during their festivals.*"

Umar also said, "*Do not learn the speech of the non-Arabs (unbelievers) and do not enter upon the polytheists in their churches during their holidays, for the wrath [of Allāh] descends upon them then.*"

It is also reported that ʿAbdullāh bin 'Amr bin Al-'Āṣ said, "*Whoever takes residence in the lands of the non-Arabs (unbelievers) and takes part in their Nayrūz and their Mahrijān (two Persian festivals) and copies them until the day he dies will be resurrected and gathered with them on the Day of Resurrection.*"

Al-Bayhaqī, Al-Sunan Al-Kubrā Vol. 9 p234.

It is reported that a man came to ʿAbdullāh bin Mas'ūd and asked, "*Teach me some comprehensive and beneficial words.*" He replied, "*Worship Allāh and do not associate any partners with Him, and be with the Qur'ān wherever it is. And whoever comes to you with some truth – whether he is young or old, even if he is hated by you – then accept [that truth]. And whoever comes lying to you – even if he is beloved and close – then reject it from him."*

Abū Bakr Al-Kharā`iṭī, Masāwī Al-Akhlāq wa Madhmūmihā p72

It is reported that Ibn Mas'ūd said, "*Whoever wants to honor his religion and do good to it should avoid mixing with the ruler or sitting with the followers of desires (heretics, people of bid'ah), for sitting with them is more contagious than scabies.*"

Ibn Wa<u>dd</u>āḥ, Al-Bida' p136.

It is reported that 'Abdullāh bin Al-Mubārak said, "*I once borrowed a pen in Al-Shām (Transjordan) and went to return it. But when I came back to Marwu (in Central Asia) I saw that I still had it, so I went back to Al-Shām to return it to its owner.*"

Al-Dhahabī, Siyar A'lām Al-Nubalā`, Vol. 8 p395.

It is reported that Sufyān Al-Thawrī said, "*Wealth is the disease of this Ummah, and the scholar is the doctor of this Ummah. So if the doctor brings the disease to himself, how will he cure the people?*"

Al-Dhahabī, Siyar A'lām Al-Nubalā`, Vol. 7 p243.

It is reported that 'Ā`ishah – said, "*Umm Ḥabībah called for me on her deathbed and said, 'There used to occur between us the kinds of things that happen between co-wives (al-ḍarā`ir), so may Allāh forgive me and you those things.' I said, 'May Allāh forgive you all those things and release you from [all liability] for that.' She replied, 'You have made me happy, may Allāh make you happy.' And she sent for Umm Salamah and said the same things to her.*"

Al-Dhahabī, Siyar A'lām Al-Nubalā` Vol. 2 p223.

It is reported that 'Alī bin Abī Ṭālib said,

"The servant [of Allāh] should not fear except his sins, and should not hope except in his Lord. The ignorant should not be ashamed to ask, and the knowledgeable should not be ashamed to say – if he does not know something – 'Allāh knows best.' Patience (al-ṣabr) to faith (Al-Īmān) is like the head to the rest of the body: if the head is cut off, the body will rot. And one who has no patience, has no faith."

Al-Baihaqī, Shu'ab Al-Īmān, Vol.12 p195.

'Uqbah bin 'Āmir Al-Juhanī once passed by a man who looked like a Muslim, so he greeted him with salām, and he replied, *"And upon you [be peace] and the mercy of Allāh and His blessings."* A boy informed him, "He is a Christian!" So 'Uqbah got up and followed the man, caught up with him and said, *"The mercy of Allāh and His blessings are upon the believers; however, may Allāh give you a long life, and make plentiful your wealth and offspring."*

Al-Bukhārī, Al-Adab Al-Mufrad.

It is reported that Ibn 'Umar said, *"We were the beginning [the heads] of this Ummah, and perhaps a man from the best of the Companions of Allāh's Messenger and the most righteous amongst them could maintain only one chapter of the Qur`ān or thereabouts. For the Qur`ān was weighty upon them, and they were given knowledge of it or action based on it. But the last of this Ummah will find the Qur`ān light [and easy] – the child and the non-Arab will recite it, without possessing any knowledge about it."*

Al-Harawī, Dhamm Al-Kalām wa Ahlihī Vol. 5 p144.

It is reported that Muḥammad bin Sīrīn said, "*They used to consider themselves on the [right] path as long as they followed al-athar (guidance of the Sunnah and Salaf as passed down in the narrations).*"

Al-Lālakā`ī, Sharḥ Usūl I'tiqād Ahl Al-Sunnah wa Al-Jamā'ah Vol.1 p120.

It is reported that 'Uthmān bin Ḥāḍir said, "I said to Ibn 'Abbās: 'advise me.' He replied, *'It is upon you to be upright, follow al-athar, and beware of innovating [in religion].'*"

Ibn Baṯṯah, Al-Ibānah Al-Kubrā Vol. 1 p214.

It is reported that ʿAbdullāh bin Al-Mubārak said, *"Let it only be the narrations (al-athar) that you rely upon, and take from reasoning and opinion that amount that will help you to understand and explain ḥadīth."*

Ibn ʿAbd Al-Barr, Jāmi' Bayān Al-'Ilm wa Faḍlihi Vol. 3 p329.

It is reported that Sufyān Al-Thawrī said, "*The narrations (al-āthār) are the religion.*"

And it is reported that he also said, "*A man should not even scratch his head except based on a narration.*"

Al-Harawī, Dhamm Al-Kalām wa Ahlihī Vol. 2 p264.

It is reported that Al-Musayyib bin Rāfi' Al-Asadī said, "*We only follow, we do not innovate; we follow behind and do not start anything [in the religion], and we will never stray as long as we adhere to the narrations.*"

Al-Harawī, Dhamm Al-Kalām wa Ahlihī Vol. 2 p265.

It is reported that Shurayḥ said, "*If I am afflicted with a calamity, I praise Allāh for it four times: I praise Him because it wasn't worse than it was, I praise Him when He gives me the patience to bear it, I praise Him for enabling me to say al-istirjā' ('To Allāh we belong and to him we will return'; see Al-Baqarah: 154-156) in hope of a great reward, and I praise Him for not making it a calamity in my religion.*"

Al-Dhahabī, Siyar A'lām Al-Nubalā`, in his biography of Shurayḥ Al-Qāḍī.

'Āṣim bin 'Umar bin Qatādah [Al-Anṣārī] reports from some men amongst his people, "*One of the things that called us to accept Islam is what we used to hear from some Jewish men. We were polytheists who worshipped idols. They (the Jews) were people of scripture and had knowledge that we did not possess. There was always some badness between us; if we did to them something they hated, they would say to us, 'The time is nigh when a Prophet will be sent, with whom we will fight and kill you like 'Ād and Iram.' We would often hear this from them. When Allāh sent His Messenger we answered him when he called us to Allāh the Exalted, and we recognized what they used to warn us about. So we preceded them to him; we believed in him and they disbelieved. And it is about us and them that these verses of Al-Baqarah were revealed: And when there came to them (the Jews), a Book (this Qur'ān) from Allāh confirming what is with them (Torah) and the Injeel, although aforetime they had invoked Allāh (for coming of the Prophet), in order to gain victory over those who disbelieved. Then when there came to them that which they recognized, they disbelieved in it. So let the curse of Allāh be on the disbelievers." [Al-Baqarah: 89]*

Ibn Hishām, Al-Sīrah Vol.1 p211, and others. Shaykh Muqbil Al-Wādi'ī graded this narrations chain of transmission ḥasan. See Al-Ṣaḥīḥ Al-Musnad min Dalā`il Al-Nubūwah p93.

It is reported that Abul-Jawzā` said, *"I would prefer to sit with swine than to sit with the people of desires (heretics, adherents of bid'ah)."*

Al-Dhahabī, Siyar A'lām Al-Nubalā`, in his biography of the Abul-Jawzā`. He reported from a number of Companions, and Al-Dhahabī considered him to be one of the senior scholars.

Ibrāhīm Al-Taymī reports from his father that Abū Dharr [Al-Ghifārī] said, *"A person possessing two dirhams will have a harsher reckoning (on the Day of Judgment) than a person who possesses just one dirham, and a person who possesses two dinars will have a harsher reckoning than someone who possesses only one."*

Ibn Al-Mubārak, Al-Zuhd wa Al-Raqā`iq article 555. Shaykh Al-Albānī graded this narration's chain of transmission ṣaḥīḥ Al-Ḍa'īfah Vol. 8 p117.

It is reported that the last sermon 'Umar bin 'Abd Al-'Aziz delivered was as follows:

He praised Allāh and said, "*You were not created in vain, nor will you be left without purpose. Verily, you have an appointed time in which Allāh – the Most High – will come down to judge you. Wretched and ruined will he be who leaves the mercy of Allāh and is denied a Garden whose width is that of the heavens and Earth. Know you not that no one will be safe tomorrow save one who is wary of today and fears it; and sells the transitory for what will remain, and the little for the plenty, and fear in exchange for security [in the hereafter]? See you not that you are in the loins of the dead, to be taken by those who remain after you, until all matters return to the Best of Inheritors? Every day, [in the funerals] you accompany those returning to Allāh the Mighty and Sublime, having spent their time, until you hide them in a crevice in the ground, in the belly of a bare and unfurnished hole, having parted from their loved ones, stroking the dirt and facing their accounts. Now, they are dependent on their deeds, free of what they left behind, in need of [the deeds] they put before them. So fear Allāh before the time He appointed is up and death descends upon you. This is what I have to say."* He then lifted the edge of his garment over his face and wept profusely, and made everyone around him weep.

Abū Bakr Al-Daynūrī, Al-Mujālasah wa Jawāhir Al-'Ilm Vol. 3 p343.

It is reported that Al-Ḥasan Al-Baṣrī used to say, "*If it were not for the munāfiqūn, you would feel all alone in the streets (the streets would be empty).*"

It is also reported that Al-Sha'bī said the same thing, "*If it were not for the munāfiqūn, you would feel all alone in the streets (the streets would be empty).*"

It is reported that Mālik bin Dīnār said, "*I swear, if the munāfiqūn started growing tails, the believers wouldn't find a spot of ground to walk on.*"

Ibn Baṯṯah, Al-Ibānah Al-Kubrā articles 936-938.

It is reported that Imām Layth bin Sa'd said, "*Even if I saw a heretic (follower of bid'ah) walk on water, I would not accept him.*" This was reported to Imām Shāfi'ī, and he said, "*He didn't go far enough. Rather, if I saw one walk in the air, I would not accept him.*"

Al-Lālakā`ī, Sharh Usūl 'I'tiqād Ahl Al-Sunnah Vol.1 p228; Ibn Battah, Al-Ibānah Al-KubrāVol2. P175; Ibn Al-Jawzī, Talbīs Iblīs p14 – with slightly variant wordings.

Mu'āwiyah bin Qurrah reports that Abū Al-Dardā` used to say, "*We ask Allāh for a lasting faith (īmān), true certainty and beneficial knowledge.*" Mu'āwiyah bin Qurrah then said, "*So this indicates that there is a type of faith that does not last, and a type of certainty that is not true, and a type of knowledge that is not beneficial.*"

Ibn Battah, Al-Ibānah Al-Kubrā Vol. 2 p498.

It is reported that Mujāhid said, "*The teacher of the kuttāb (where the children would be taught, the madrasah) will be brought on the Day of Resurrection, and if he was not fair and just with the boys, he will be grouped with the tyrants.*"

Abū Bakr Al-Daynūrī, Al-Mujālasah wa Jawāhir Al-'Ilm article 619.

It is reported that Hammād bin Salamah said, "*Being cursed (al-la'nah) is not some blackness that can be seen in the face, but it is when you do not leave a sin without falling into another.*"

Abū Bakr Al-Daynūrī, Al-Mujālasah wa Jawāhir Al-'Ilm article 765.

It is reported that Imām Ayyūb [Al-Sakhtiyānī] said, "*When I hear of the death of a man from Ahl Al-Sunnah, it is as if I have lost a part of my body.*"

Al-Lālakā`ī, Shar<u>h</u> Usūl I'tiqād Ahl Al-Sunnah wa Al-Jamā'ah, Vol.1 p46.

It is reported that <u>H</u>ammād bin Zayd said, "*When the news of the death of a young man from the followers of <u>h</u>adīth reached Ayyūb, [the sorrow] could be seen on him; and when the news of the death of a man who was mentioned as being a devout worshipper would reach him, [it's effect] on him was not noticed.*"

Al-Lālakā`ī, Shar<u>h</u> Usūl I'tiqād Ahl Al-Sunnah wa Al-Jamā'ah, Vol.1 p51.

It is also reported that <u>H</u>ammād bin Zayd said, "*I was with Ayyūb Al-Sakhtiyānī while he was washing [the body] of Shu'ayb bin Al-<u>H</u>ab<u>h</u>āb, saying, 'Anyone who wishes for the death of a person from Ahl Al-Sunnah has wished for the light of Allāh to be extinguished; but Allāh will keep His light complete, even though the unbelievers may hate it.' [Sūrah Al-<u>S</u>aff: 8]*"

Al-Lālakā`ī, Shar<u>h</u> Usūl I'tiqād Ahl Al-Sunnah wa Al-Jamā'ah, Vol.1 p52.

It is reported that Asad bin Mūsā said, "*We were with Sufyān bin 'Uyainah when he was informed of the death of Al-Darāwardī, and he became visibly distressed. [Al-Darāwardī] hadn't actually died, so we said, 'We didn't think you would reach such a state.' He said, '[Al-Darāwardī] is from Ahl Al-Sunnah.'*"

Al-Lālakā'ī, Shar<u>h</u> Usūl I'tiqad Ah̞l Al Sunnah wa Al-Jamā'ah, Vol.1 p72.

It is reported that Abū Hurayrah said, "*People say, 'Abū Hurayrah reports so many [<u>h</u>adīth],' but if it were not for two verses in Allāh's book, I would not narrate a single <u>h</u>adīth.*" Then he recited, "*Verily, those who hide what Allāh has sent down of the Book (Al-Baqarah: 174),*" and "*Verily, those who hide what We have sent down of clear explanation and guidance. (Al-Baqarah: 159)*" He then said, "*Our brothers, the Muhājirūn, used to be occupied with trading in the markets, and our brothers, the An<u>s</u>ār, would be occupied with dealing with their wealth and property, but Abū Hurayrah used to stay with Allāh's Messenger for his fill, and would be present when they were not.*"

This wording has been reported by Al-<u>H</u>āfidh Ibn ʿAbd Al-Barr, Jāmi' Bayān Al-ʿIlm Vol.1 p464.

Commenting on this narration, Ibn ʿAbd Al-Barr states, "*In this narration there are a number of meanings to understand, including: The <u>h</u>adīth from Allāh's Messenger has the same ruling as the revealed Book of Allāh. Knowledge should be shown, spread and taught. One should stick with the scholars. One should be satisfied with the little he can get of worldly provision in order to pursue his desire for knowledge. One should prefer knowledge over being occupied with worldly pursuits and income.*

It is reported that Abū Al-Dardā' used to say, "*Learn knowledge before it is taken way, and it is taken away by its people (scholars) being taken away. The scholar and the student are partners in good and there is no good in any other people. The richest of men is the knowledgeable man whose knowledge is needed: he benefits those who need him and if done without, he benefits himself with the knowledge Allāh has placed with him. So how is it I see your scholars dying yet the ignorant amongst you not learning? I fear that the predecessor will depart and the successor will not learn. If the scholar studies, he only increases in knowledge, and he does not take anything away from knowledge. And if the ignorant studies, he will find knowledge firm and established. So how is it that I see you full up with food, yet starved of knowledge?"*

Ibn ʿAbd Al-Barr, Jāmi' Bayān Al-'Ilm wa Fa<u>d</u>lihi Vol. 2 p233.

It is reported on the authority of Ibrāhīm bin Al-Ash'ath that he said, *"I asked Al-Fu<u>d</u>ayl bin ʿAyyāḍ about patience (al-<u>s</u>abr) in the face of adversity and he said, 'It is to not broadcast it.' I asked him about asceticism (al-zuhd) and he said, 'Al-zuhd is to be content with what you have, and that is what it means to be rich.' I asked him about prudence (al-wara') and he said, 'It is to stay away from what is forbidden.' And I asked him about humbleness (al-tawā<u>d</u>u') and he said, 'It is when you submit to the truth and comply no matter who you hear it from; even if it was from the most ignorant of people, you would be required to accept it from him.'"*

Ibn ʿAbd Al-Barr, Jāmi' Bayān Al-'Ilm wa Fa<u>d</u>lihi Vol. 1 p498.

Abū Hurayrah once saw two men. He asked one of them, "How is this man related to you?" He replied, "He is my father." Abū Hurayrah said, *"Do not call him by his name, do not walk in front of him and do not sit before he does."*

Al-Bukhārī, Al-Adab Al-Mufrad. It is reported from Al-<u>H</u>asan Al-Ba<u>s</u>rī that he said, *"If a man from amongst the Salaf were to be sent forth today, he would not recognize anything from Islam." He put his hand on his cheek and added, "Except this prayer (salāh)." Then he said, "But by Allāh, this does not apply to the person who lives in this unfamiliar time, never having seen the Righteous Predecessors, but who sees [instead] the innovator calling to his bid'ah, and the follower of worldly wealth calling to his materialism, but Allāh protects him from all this and makes his heart love and aspire to those Righteous Predecessors, asking about their way, searching and trying to follow in their footsteps, and adhering to their path. Such is a person who will be recompensed with an immense and great reward. So be you all like this, by Allāh's permission".*

Ibn Waddāh, Al-Bida' Vol. 1 p190.

It is reported from Hibbān bin Abī Jablah that he said, "*The women of this world who enter Paradise will surpass Al-Hūr Al-'Īn by the deeds they did in this world.*"

Ibn Al-Mubārak, Al-Zuhd wa Al-Raqā`iq Vol. 4 p463.

Hibbān bin Abī Jablah is from the Tābi'ūn. He died in 122 or 125H.

It is reported that 'Amr bin Qays – Al-Malā`ī said, "*They used to dislike a man giving his child something with which the child would then go out and be seen by a poor person, causing him to cry over his family; or be seen by an orphan who would then cry over his family.*"

Imām Ahmad, Al-Zuhd Vol. 3 p268.

'Amr bin Qays Al-Malā`ī lived in the time of the younger Tābi'ūn. He died in 146H.

It is reported that Al-Fu<u>d</u>ayl bin ʿAyyāḍ said, "*When backbiting appears, brotherhood for Allāh will disappear; and at that time you will be like things plated with gold and silver: wooden on the inside, [merely] looking good on the outside.*"

Abū Nu'aym, <u>H</u>ilyah Al-Awliyā`, Vol. 3 p395.

It is reported that if Hishām Al-Dustawā`ī didn't have a torch on at home, he would toss and turn in bed until his wife would come with a torch. She asked him about this once, and he said, "*If I don't have a torch, I think about the darkness of the grave.*"

Al-Dhahabī, Siyar A'lām Al-Nubalā`, in his biography of Hishām Al-Dustawā`ī.

It is reported that Hishām bin 'Urwah said, reporting from his father, 'Urwah bin Al-Zubayr, "*He used to say to us when we were youths, 'Why do you not seek knowledge? Even though [today] you are the youngsters, you are about to be the elders [in the future]. What is the use of being a shaykh when the shaykh is ignorant? Four years before the death of 'Ā`ishah, I would say, if she died today, I would not feel regret about a single <u>h</u>adīth she had, for I had gathered them from her. I would hear that a Companion had a <u>h</u>adīth and would go to him. I might find that he was napping, so I would sit at his door and wait, and then ask him about it [later when he woke].'*"

Al-Dhahabī, Siyar A'lām Al-Nubalā`, in his biography of 'Urwah bin Al-Zubayr.

It is reported that Mu<u>h</u>ammad Al-Bāqir said,

"*Never does any pride enter the heart of a man except that his intelligence decreases by the same amount.*"

Al-Dhahabī, Siyar A'lām Al-Nubalā`, in his biography of Muhammad Al-Bāqir.

Imām Ahmad said, "*The graves of Ahl Al-Sunnah who committed major sins are gardens (from Paradise) whilst the graves of the heretics (adherents of Bid'ah) who were ascetics are pits (from the Fire). The sinners from Ahl Al-Sunnah are the beloved (awliyā`) of Allāh, whereas the ascetics of Ahl Al-Bid'ah are the enemies of Allāh.*"

Ibn Abī Ya'lā, Tabaqāt Al-Hanābilah Vol. 1 p182.

Al-Sha'bī reports, "*When the Companions of Muhammad used to meet, they would shake hands; and when returning from travels, they would hug one another.*"

Shaykh Al-Albānī states in Al-Sahīhah Vol. 1 p300, "[This is] recorded by Al-Bayhaqī Vol. 7 p100 with a sahīh chain of transmission from Al-Sha'bī."

Abū Madīnah Al-Dārimī reports, "*When two of the Companions of Allāh's Messenger would meet, they would not part until one would recite to the other "By time, verily man is in loss..." (Sūrah Al-'Asr). Then, one of them would say salām to the other.*"

Recorded by Al-Tabarānī in Al-Awsat, and others. Shaykh Al-Albānī graded its chain of transmission sahīh. See Al-Sahīhah, hadīth 2648.

Shaykh Al-Albānī states, "There are two points of benefit in this narration about the practice of our Salaf. The first is that they used to say salām when parting, which has been explicitly mentioned in some statements of the Prophet...The other, we learn from the regular practice of the Companions, is reciting

Sūrah Al-'Asr [when parting], for we believe that they were the farthest of people from introducing into the religion a worship by which they sought to bring themselves closer to Allāh, except with some sanction from Allāh's Messenger – peace and blessings be upon him, either through a statement from him, or an action of his, or by his tacit approval..."

ʿAbdullāh bin Mas'ūd said,

"Verily, Allāh looked inside the hearts of people and found the heart of Muhammad to be the best of all hearts, and so He chose him for Himself and sent him with His message. Then Allāh looked inside the hearts of people after Muhammad and found the hearts of his Companions to be the best hearts; so He made them the ministers and representatives of His Prophet, fighting for his religion. Thus, what the Muslims regard as good is good with Allāh, and what they regard as evil is evil with Allāh. And the Companions unanimously chose to take Abū Bakr as the successor [to lead the Muslims after the Prophet]."

Reported by Ahmad, Al-Tayālisī and others, excluding the last sentence. Shaykh Al-Albānī graded its chain of transmission hasan. The narration is reported with the last sentence by Al-Hākim, who said its chain of transmission is sahīh. Al-Dhahabī agrees, while Al-Hāfidh Al-Sakhāwī said, "It is mawqūf (reported as a statement of a Companion), hasan." See Al-Albānī, Al-Da'īfah Vol. 2 pp17-19.

Al-Hāfidh Ibn ʿAbd Al-Barr states in Jāmi' Bayān Al-'Ilm Vol. 2 p36, 37, *"The definition of knowledge according to the scholars is whatever a person is clear and sure about. Anyone who is certain and clear about something knows it. Therefore, whoever is not certain about something but says it blindly following someone else, does not know it. Blind following is – according to the scholars – different from following (al-ittibā'). Because following is to follow a person based on what has become clear to you of the correctness of his position, whereas blind-following is to say what he says while not understanding it or its reasoning."*

It is reported that Sufyān bin 'Uyainah said, "*The intelligent person is not one who merely knows what is good and what is bad. The intelligent person is one who, when he sees what is good, follows it, and when he sees evil, shuns it."*

Abū Nu'aym, H̲ilyah Al-Awliyā`, Vol. 4 p16.

It is reported that 'Abdullāh bin 'Abbās said, "*Love for Allāh and hate for Allāh, make your enmity because of Allāh and your allegiance because of Allāh; for indeed, the love and support of Allāh is not achieved save through this. And a man will never taste true faith (īmān) – though he may pray and fast much – except when he is like that. Today, the people's brotherhood is based upon worldly considerations (dunyā), but this will not do anything for them on the Day of Resurrection."*

Ibn Al-Mubārak, Al-Zuhd wa Al-Raqā`iq article 353.

It is reported from Abū Al-Dardā that he said,

"Three make me laugh, and three make me cry.

Those that make me laugh are a person who puts his hopes in this worldly life while death pursues him, a person who is heedless [of his Lord] while [his Lord] is not heedless of him, and a person who always laughs while he does not know whether he has pleased Allāh or angered Him.

What makes me cry is being separated from my beloved: Muhammad and his party (the Companions), the horrors of the time of death, and standing in front of Allāh on the Day when the secrets will be revealed and I do not know will I then go to Paradise or Hell?"

Ibn Al-Mubārak, Al-Zuhd wa Al-Raqā`iq article 250.

It is reported that 'Alī bin Ḥusayn said,

"Tawbah(repentance) is only through action, and turning back from what has been done. Tawbah is not by mere speech."

Ibn Abī Al-Dunyā, Al-Tawbah article 57.

It was said to Al-Ḥasan Al-Baṣrī,

"People say that the one who has been on Ḥajj is the one who is forgiven." He said, "And the sign of this is that he leaves the evils he used to do."

Ibn Abī Al-Dunyā, Al-Tawbah article 70.

It is reported that Ṭalq bin Ḥabīb said,

"The right of Allāh is too great and heavy for the creation to fulfill and the blessings of Allāh are too many to enumerate, but you should remain repentant, morning and evening."

Ibn Abī Al-Dunyā, Al-Tawbah article 62.

It is reported that Al-Sha'bī said,

"The only people who used to seek this knowledge were those who combined two characteristics: intelligence and devout worship. If a person was intelligent but not devout, it would be said that only the worshippers can attain this [knowledge], and

so he would not try to seek it. And if a person was devout, but not intelligent, it would be said that only the intelligent can attain this [knowledge], and so he would not try to seek it." Al-Sha'bī continued, *"And I fear that today, people who are neither intelligent nor devout try to seek it."*

Ibn Ḥibbān Al-Bustī, Rawḍatu Al-'Uqalā` wa Nuzhatu Al-Fuḍalā` Vol.1 p9.

It is reported that Al-Fuḍayl bin 'Ayyāḍ said, *"If I had one supplication that was going to be answered I would make it for the ruler (imām), for the wellbeing and righteousness of the imām means wellbeing for the land and its people."*

Al-Dhahabī, Siyar A'lām Al-Nubalā` in his biography of Al-Fuḍayl bin 'Ayyāḍ.

It is reported that Muḥammad bin Sīrīn said, *"I have never envied anyone over anything: if a person is going to be in the Fire, how could I envy him over some worldly matter when he is destined for the Fire?! And if he is going to Paradise, how could I be envious of a man of Paradise with whom Allāh is pleased?!" Muslim said, "We have never heard anything better than this from the words of Ibn Sīrīn."*

Abū Bakr Al-Daynūrī, Al-Mujālasah wa Jawāhir Al-'Ilm article 2931.

The great ascetic Shaqīq Al-Balakhī was once asked, "*What is the mark of [true] repentance*?" He replied, "*Continued crying over past sins, deep fear of falling into them again, staying away from bad company, and keeping the company of good people.*"

Abū Bakr Al-Daynūrī, Al-Mujālasah wa Jawāhir Al-'Ilm article 2645.

It is reported that Abū Bakr Al-Ṣiddīq said,

"One of the worst sins is a person taking his sin lightly."

Abū Bakr Al-Daynūrī, Al-Mujālasah wa Jawāhir Al-'Ilm article 2318.

It is reported that ʿAbdullāh bin Mas'ūd said,

"One of the worst sins is when a man says to his brother, "Fear Allāh,' and he replies, "Worry about yourself."

Abū Bakr Al-Daynūrī, Al-Mujālasah wa Jawāhir Al-'Ilm article 2619.

It is reported that Bashr bin Al-H̲ārith said, *"I was once with Al-Fuḍayl bin ʿAyyāḍ in Makkah. He sat with us until midnight, then went and did ṭawāf until the morning. I said, 'Abū 'Alī! Won't you sleep?' He replied, 'Woe to you! And is there anyone who hears a mention of the Fire and then feels like sleeping!?'"*

Abū Bakr Al-Daynūrī, Al-Mujālasah wa Jawāhir Al-'Ilm, article 723.

It is reported that a group of heretics (People of Bid'ah) and their devout worship was mentioned to ʿAbd Al-Raḥmān bin Mahdī. He said, *"Allāh only accepts what conforms to what has been commanded and what is in the Sunnah."* Then he recited, And a monasticism which they (Christians) innovated, We did not ordain it upon them [Al-Ḥadīd: 27]. He went on to say, *"So Allāh did not accept this from them and reprimanded them for it."* He then said, *"Stick to the way and the Sunnah."*

Abū Nu'aym, Ḥilyah Al-Awliyā` Vol.4 p44.

It is reported that Makḥūl said, "*The people with the softest hearts are those who sin the least.*"

Abū Nu'aym, Ḥilyah Al-Awliyā` Vol. 2 p344.

It is reported that 'Awn bin ʿAbdillāh, the ascetic and jurist, said, "*Sit with the repentant, for they have the softest hearts.*"

Abū Nu'aym, Ḥilyah Al-Awliyā` Vol. 2 p192.

Al-Ṭufayl bin Ubay bin Ka'b narrated that he used to come to ʿAbdullāh bin ʿUmar and go with him to the market. He said, "*Whenever we went to the market, ʿAbdullāh bin ʿUmar would never pass a cheap goods merchant, a seller, a poor person or anyone else except that he would greet them with salāms.*" He continued, "*So I came to him one day and he asked me to go to the market with him. I said, 'And what are you going to do at the market? You never stop to buy anything, you never ask about goods, you never price anything and you never sit in the market gatherings. Sit with us here and we can talk. So he said to me, 'O Abū Baṭn (i.e. possessor of the belly; Al-Ṭufayl had a big belly)! We only go out for salāms, to greet those we meet.''*"

Al-Bukhārī, Al-Adab Al-Mufrad, Al-Albānī's Ṣaḥīḥ Al-Adab Al-Mufrad Vol. 1 p395.

It is reported that Al-Awzāʿī said:

"Follow the narrations [ways] of those who have preceded (the Salaf) even if people reject you; and beware of people's opinions, even if they beautify them for you."

Al-Ājurrī, Kitāb Al-Sharīʿah 1:138; Ibn ʿAbd Al-Barr, Jāmiʿ Bayān Al-ʿIlm wa Faḍlihi 3:373.

Ma'an bin 'Īsā reports Imām Mālik said,

"I am but a man. I make mistakes sometimes and I am correct sometimes, so examine my opinions and accept anything that agrees with the Book and Sunnah; and leave anything that does not agree with the Book and Sunnah."

Ibn ʿAbd Al-Barr, Jāmi' Bayān Al-'Ilm wa Faḍlihi Vol.2 p465.

It is reported that Imām Mālik said:

I heard Rabīʿah bin ʿAbd Al-Raḥmān say,

"The people under the care of their scholars are like children in the laps of their fathers."

Ibn Baṭṭah, Al-Ibānah Al-Kubrā ḥadīth 40.

It is reported that Abū Ayyūb Al-Anṣārī said,

"A person might do a single good deed, rely on it and forget sins that he regards insignificant, but then meet Allāh (on the Day of Judgment) with those sins surrounding him. And a man might commit a sin, but never stop fearing its consequences, until he meets Allāh safe and sound."

Al-Ḥāfidh Ibn Ḥajr, Fatḥ Al-Bārī, references this narration to Asad bin Mūsā's Al-Zuhd. A slightly different wording is reported by Ibn Al-Mubārak in Al-Zuhd wa Al-Raqā`iq Vol.1 p170.

It is reported that Ṭāwūs said, *"The worship and devoutness of a young person is not complete until he marries."* Ibrāhīm bin

Maysurah reports that Ṭawūs said to him, "*You better get married or I will say to you what 'Umar bin Al-Khaṯṯāb said to Abū Al-Zawā`id: 'Nothing but incapability or sinfulness is preventing you from getting married!'*"

Al-Dhahabī, Siyar A'lām Al-Nubalā`, in his biography of Ṭāwūs.

It is reported that 'Umar bin 'Abd Al-'Azīz once wrote to Al-Ḥasan Al-Baṣrī to get a brief exhortation from him, so Al-Ḥasan wrote back , "*The dunyā distracts and preoccupies the heart and body, but al-zuhd (asceticism, not giving importance to worldly things) gives rest to the heart and body. Verily, Allāh will ask us about the ḥalāl things we enjoyed, so what about the ḥarām!*"

Al-Bayhaqī, Al-Zuhd Al-Kabīr, article 26.

It is reported that Al-Ḥasan Al-Baṣrī often used to say,

"*O youth! Seek the hereafter, for we often see people pursuing the hereafter and finding it as well as the dunyā (worldly wellbeing), but we have never seen anyone pursue the dunyā and gain the hereafter as well as the dunyā.*"

Al-Bayhaqī, Al-Zuhd Al-Kabīr, article 12.

One of the reported instructions 'Umar wrote to Abū Mūsā Al-Ash'arī and those under his governance during the former's Caliphate was, "*Seek knowledge and understanding of (fiqh) the Sunnah and seek knowledge and understanding of Arabic.*"

Ibn Abī Shaybah, Al-Muṣannaf Vol.6 p126.

It is reported that Umar said, "*Learn Arabic, for it strengthens the intelligence and increases one's noble conduct (al-murū`ah).*"

Al-Bayhaqī, Shu'ab Al-Īmān Vol.4 p187.

It is also reported that Umar bin khattab was once circumambulating the Ka'bah when he heard two men speaking in a language other than Arabic behind him. He turned to them and said, "*Find some way to learn Arabic.*"

ʿAbd Al-Razzāq Al-Ṣan'ānī, Al-Muṣannaf Vol.5 p496.

It is reported Ubay bin Ka'b said,

"Learn Arabic just as you learn to memorize the Qurān."

Ibn Abī Shaybah, Al-Muṣannaf Vol.7 p150.

It is reported that Shu'bah said,

"Learn Arabic, for it increases the intelligence."

Tahdhīb Al-Tahdhīb Vol.4 p303.

It is reported that 'Attā bin Abī Rabāḥ said, "*I wish I were fluent in Arabic,*" when he was ninety years old.

Al-Dhahabī, Siyar A'lām Al-Nubalā`, in his biography of 'Attā bin Abī Rabāh.

It is reported that Ibn Shubrumah said, "*Men have never worn a garment more beautiful than Arabic.*"

Al-Bayhaqī, Shu'ab Al-Īmān Vol.4 p197.

A man once asked 'Alī about taking a full bath (ghusl). He replied, "*Wash every day if you want.*" The man said, "No, what I mean is the ghusl." ʿAli replied, *"Al-Jumu'ah (Friday), the Day of 'Arafah, the Day of Al-Naḥr (sacrificial slaughter, 'Eid al-Adhā) and the Day of Al-Fiṭr (the 'Eid following Ramaḍān)."*

Al-Bayhaqī, Al-Sunan Al-Kubrā, ḥadīth #6343. In Irwā Al-Ghalīl, under ḥadīth #146, Shaykh Al-Albānī graded its chain of transmission ṣaḥīḥ and said this is the best evidence for the recommendation to bath on the two 'Eid celebrations.

It is reported that 'Abdullāh bin Al-Mubārak was criticized for spending on [other people in] other lands and not his own. In response, he said, "*I know the locations of virtuous, sincere and truthful people who seek and study ḥadīth and do it well because people are in need of them. They are needy, and if we leave them, their knowledge will be lost; but if we help them, they will spread knowledge to the Ummah of Muḥammad – Allāh's. I do not know of anything more virtuous, after Prophecy, than spreading knowledge.*"

Al-Dhahabī, Siyar A'lām Al-Nubalā`, in his biography of 'Abdullāh bin Al-Mubārak.

The Companions of Allāh's Messenger used to say to each other when they met on 'Eid:

تَقَبَّلَ اللّٰهُ مِنَّا وَ مِنْكُمْ

(taqabbalallāhu minnā wa minkum, which means 'may Allāh accept from us and you [our fasts and deeds].')

Al-Ḥāfidh Ibn Ḥajr, Fatḥ Al-Bārī, grades this narration's chain of transmission ḥasan and cites it from Al-Maḥāmilīyyāt.

It is reported from Ka'b Al-Aḥbār that he said:

"Allāh chose from the months the month of Ramaḍān, from all the lands He chose Makkah, from the nights He chose Laylatu Al-Qadr (The Night of Decree), and chose the times for prayers; so a believer is always between two good deeds: one he has done and the other he is waiting to do."

Abū Nu'aym, Ḥilyah Al-Awliyā` Vol.2 p458.

Ma'n bin 'Īsā reports

Mālik bin Anas was once returning from the mosque, leaning on my arm, when a man called Abū Al-Juwayrīyah who was accused of Al-Irjā` caught up with him. He said. *"O Abū 'Abdullāh, listen to something I have to say and debate with me and let me tell you my opinion."* [Imām] Mālik said, *"And what if you overcome me?"* The man replied, *"If I defeat you, you follow me."* Mālik asked, *"And what if another man comes and defeats us?"* He replied, *"Then we follow him."* To this, Mālik said, *"O servant of Allāh, Allāh sent Muḥammad with a single religion, but I see you moving from religion to religion. 'Umar bin 'Abd Al-'Azīz said, 'Whoever makes his religion the object of argumentation will frequently change it.'"*

Al-Ājurrī, Ktāb Al-Sharī'ah Vol.1 p128.

It is reported that Ma'rūf Al-Kar<u>kh</u>ī said:

"When Allāh chooses good for a person He opens the door to action for him, and closes the door to argumentation; and when Allāh chooses evil for a person he opens the door of argumentation and closes the door to action."

Al-<u>Kh</u>aṭīb Al-Baghdādī, Iqtḍā Al-'Ilm Al-'Amal, article 123.

Ka'b Al-A<u>h</u>bār said:

"I would rather fornicate thirty-three times than consume a dirham of usury while Allāh knows that I knowingly consumed it as usury,"

Al-Mundhirī states in Al-Targhīb wa Al-Tarhīb, "Reported by Ahmad through a good chain of transmitters." Graded sahīh by Al-Albāni in Sahīh Al-Targhīb wa Al-Tarhīb Vol. 2 p178.

Maytham, a Companion of Allāh's Messenger said:

"It has reached me that an angel goes out, holding his flag, with the first person to go to the masjid and stays holding his flag with him until he returns and then enters his home with it. And Shayṭān goes out, holding his flag, with the first person to go to the market and stays holding his flag with him until he returns and puts it in his home."

Al-Mundhirī states in Al-Targhīb wa Al-Tarhīb, "Reported by Ibn Abī 'Āṣim amd Abū Nu'aym in Ma'rifatu Al-Ṣaḥābah and other works." Graded ṣaḥīḥ by Al-Albāni in Ṣaḥīḥ Al-Targhīb wa Al-Tarhīb 1:101.

O Believers! Repent to Allāh truly and sincerely [Al-Taḥrīm (66): 8]

In explanation of this verse, Al-Ṭabarī reports the following narrations in his Tafsīr:

He reports that 'Umar bin Al-Khattāb was asked about true repentance. He replied, "*It is that a man repents from an evil deed, and never does it again.*" He also reports that 'Umar said, "*It is that you repent from the sin and never do it again, or never intend to do it again.*" Similarly, he reports from 'Abdullāh (Ibn 'Abbās) that he said, "*A person repents, and then never goes back to the sin."*, and *"It means that a person never returns to the sin from which he repented."*

Mujāhid is quoted as saying, *"They seek Allāh's forgiveness and then never go back to sin."*

Qatādah is quoted as saying, *"It is the true and sincere repentance."*

Al-Ṭabarī, Tafsīr Al-Ṭabarī, in the commentary on Sūrah Al-Taḥrīm.

ʿAbdullāh bin 'Amr said:

"It would be better for a person to be turned to dust than to deliberately walk in front of a person who is praying."

Ibn ʿAbd Al-Barr, Al-Tamhīd. Graded s̲ah̲īh̲ by Shaykh Al-Albānī in S̲ah̲īh̲ Al-Targhībi wa Al-Tarhīb Vol. 1 p135.

ʿAbdullah bin Mas'ūd said:

"Falling asleep when remembering Allāh is from Shayṭān; if you want you can test this: when you lie down and want to fall asleep, try remembering Allāh."

Al-Bukhārī, Al-Adab Al-Mufrad. Graded ṣaḥīḥ by Shaykh Al-Albānī in Ṣaḥīḥ Al-Adab Al-Mufrad Vol. 1 p490.

Al-H̲āfidh Ibn Kathīr reports the following incident in his tafsīrof Sūrah Al-Jinn, verse 11:

ʿAbdullāh bin Mas'ūd said:

"Women are but an 'awrah (something private to be covered). A woman might leave her house without there being any problem with her, but the Shayt̲ān seeks her out and says [to her], "You

will not pass by anyone except that you will impress/please him."
A woman puts on her clothes and is asked where she is going, to
which she replies, "To visit a sick person," or "to attend a
funeral", or "to pray in the masjid"; but a woman never worships
Allāh in the way she does when she worships Him in her house."

Al-Ṭabarānī. Graded ṣaḥīḥ by Shaykh Al-Albānī in Ṣaḥīḥ Al-
Targhībi wa Al-Tarhīb Vol. 1 p84.

ʿAbdullāh bin ʿAmr said:

"Killing a believer is worse to Allāh than the ending of the world."

Al-Nasā`ī, Al-Sunan. Graded ṣaḥīḥ by Shaykh Al-Albānī
in Ṣaḥīḥ Al-Jāmiʿ no.4361.

ʿAbdullāh bin Masʿūd said:

"A believer might harbour any [bad] quality, except treachery
and lying."

Ibn Abī Shaybah, Kitāb Al-Īmān article 80, where Al-Albānī
grades its chain of narration ṣaḥīḥ; and others.

Saʿd bin Abī Waqqās said:

"A believer might be characterised with any [bad] quality, except
treachery and lying."

Ibn Abī Shaybah, Kitāb Al-Īmān article 81, where Al-Albānī
grades its chain of narration ṣaḥīḥ; and others.

ʿAbdul-Awwal narrates that he heard his father Hammaad ibn
Muhammad al-Ansaaree say:

Whoever falls into an innovation, it is said to him:

"This action of yours is an innovation".

And if he persists in this (innovation), then it is said to him:

"You are an innovator (mubtadi')."

al-Majmoo' fee Tarjamatil-Muhaddith Hammaad ibn Muhammad al-Ansaaree wa Seeratuhu wa Aqwaalauhu – Volume 2, Quote No.39, Page 482

Muhammad bin Ziyâd said, *"I met [some of] the Salaf. They would live in one building with their families. One of them might receive guests, and the cooking pot of another might be on the fire (with food being cooked). The host would take the pot to serve his guest, and the owner of the pot would find it had gone and would ask, "Who has taken the pot?" The host would reply, "We have taken it for our guest." The owner would say, "May Allâh bless it for you," or something similar. Baqîyah (one of the reporters) said, "Muhammad said, 'And it was the same when they baked bread; and they had only a wall of reeds separating them in those days.'" Baqîyah added, "And I remember seeing such times with Muhammad bin Ziyâd and his friends.""*

Al-Bukhârî, Al-Adab Al-Mufrad. Shaykh Al-Albânî (Sahîh Al-Adab Al-Mufrad p268) said this narration's chain of narration is sahîh.

'Amr bin Al-'Âs was once walking with a group of his friends, when he passed by the bloated, rotting carcass of mule. He said: *"By Allah! To eat your fill from this carcass is better than eating the flesh of a Muslim (by backbiting him)."*

Al-Bukhârî, Al-Adab Al-Mufrad. Shaykh Al-Albânî (Sahîh Al-Adab Al-Mufrad p266) said this narration's chain of narration is sahîh.

On the authority of ʿAbdullāh Ibn Mas'ūd, who said:

"May Allāh curse those women who tattoo or seek to be tattooed, those women who remove facial hair or seek it to be removed and those women who put gaps between their teeth for beautification; those who seek to change Allāh's creation."

This reached a woman from Banī Asad who was called Umm Ya'qūb and who used to read the Qur`ān. She came to [Ibn Mas'ūd] and said, "*What is this I hear from you, that you curse women who tattoo or seek to get tattooed, and those who remove facial hair and those who put gaps between their teeth for beauty, those who change Allāh's creation?"* ʿAbdullāh [Ibn Mas'ūd] replied, "*And why should I not curse those whom Allāh's Messenger has cursed and those who are mentioned in Allāh's Book?"* She said, "*I have read [the Qur`ān] from cover to cover and I have not seen it mentioned.*" He replied, "*If you had really read it [carefully] you would have found it; Allāh the Mighty and Sublime said: And whatever the Messenger gives you, take it; and whatever he forbids you, shun it. [Al-Ḥashr (59):7]*

The woman then said, "*Well I have just seen some of this on your own wife.*" He said, "*Go and see her.*" So she went to the wife of ʿAbdullāh but didn't see anything. She returned to him and said, "*I don't see anything.*" He said, "*Well, if any of those practices had been done I would not be with her any more.*"

Al-Bukhārī and Muslim. This translation is from the version in Muslim.

It is reported from Al-Awzâ'î that he said:

I have been told that it used to be said, "Woe to those who study [their religion] for a purpose other than worship, and those who seek to permit what is forbidden through doubts and specious arguments."

Al-Khattîb Al-Baghdâdî, Iqtdâ Al-'Ilm Al-'Amal, p77.

Umm Al-Dardâ` [the Younger] reports:

One day, Abû Al-Dardâ` came home angry, so I asked him, "What has made you so angry?" He replied, "By Allâh, I do not recognize anything from the Ummah of Muhammad except that they pray (salâh) in congregation."

Al-Bukhârî, Al-Sahîh, Chapter on the Virtue of Praying Al-Fajr in Congregation.

It is reported that Al-Fuḍayl bin ʿAyyāḍ said:

"If you can be unknown, be so; it doesn't matter if you are not known and it doesn't matter if you are not praised. It doesn't matter if you are blameworthy according to people if you are praiseworthy with Allāh the Mighty and Majestic."

Al-Bayhaqī, Al-Zuhd Al-Kabīr p100.

O People of Scripture! Do not be extreme in your religion! [Al-Mâ`idah (5): 77]

It is reported from Qatâdah that he said, commenting on this verse, "*Meaning: do not innovate in religion and do not sit with a religious innovator (mubtadi')*."

Ibn Battah, Al-Ibânah Al-Kubrâ Vol.1 p394.

It is reported from Abû Qilâbah that he said:

"Do not sit with the People of Desires (Bid'ah), for I fear that they will immerse you in their misguidance or mix up and confuse what you already know."

Ibn Ba<u>tt</u>ah, Al-Ibânah Al-Kubrâ Vol.1 p377.

It is reported from Al-<u>H</u>asan Al-Ba<u>s</u>rî that he said:

"The life of this world is made up of three days: yesterday has gone with all that was done; tomorrow, you may never reach; but today is for you so do what you should do today."

Al-Bayhaqî, Al-Zuhd Al-Kabîr p197.

A man once asked Abū Hurayrah, '*What is al-taqwā?"* He replied, "*Have you ever taken a path filled with thorns?"* The man replied, "*I have."* Abū Hurayrah asked him, "*What did you do?"* He replied, "*When I saw a thorn I would dodge it or pass over it or behind it.*" Abū Hurayrah said, "*That is al-taqwā.*"

Al-Baihaqī, Al-Zuhd Al-Kabīr p351.

It is reported from Al-<u>H</u>asan Al-Ba<u>s</u>rî that he said:

"It used to be said: it is part of al-nifâq (hypocrisy) to be inwardly different from what you are on the outside, to say one thing and do another and to be different in how you enter and how you leave. And the root of al-nifâq is lying."

Abû Bakr Al-Kharâ`i<u>t</u>î, Masâwî Al-Akhlâq wa Madhmûmihâ p62

It is reported from Nu'aym bin <u>H</u>ammâd:

'Abdullah bin Al-Mubârak used to often stay at home, so he was asked, "*Don't you get lonely?*" He replied, "*How could I get lonely when I am with the Prophet (i.e. I read his hadîth)?*"

Also on the authority of Nu'aym bin Hammâd:

It was once said to 'Abdullah bin Al-Mubârak, "*O Abû 'Abd Al-Rahmân, you often sit alone at home.*" He said, "*I am alone? I am with the Prophet and his Companions.*" Meaning: reading hadîth.

Ibn 'Asâkir, Târîkh Dimishq Vol. 32 p458.

Shaqîq bin Ibrâhîm reports:

It was once said to 'Abdullah bin Al-Mubârak, "*After you have prayed with us you don't sit with us?*" He replied, "*I go and sit with the Sahâbah and the Tâbi'în.*" We said, "*And how can you sit with the Sahâbah and Tâbi'în (when they have all passed away)?*" He replied, "*I go and read the knowledge I have collected, I find their narrations and deeds. What would I do with you? You sit around backbiting people.*"

Al-Dhahabî, Siyar A'lâm Al-Nubalâ` in his biography of 'Abdullah bin Al-Mubârak.

Imâm Al-Awzâ'î said:

"We used to say – while the Tâbi'ûn were abundant – that Allâh is above his 'Arsh (Throne), and we believe in what is present in the Sunnah about His attributes."

Al-Baihaqî, Al-Asmâ` wa Al-Sifât and Al-Dhahabî, Siyar A'lâm Al-Nubalâ` in his biography of Al-Awzâ'î.

It is reported from Imâm Sufyân bin 'Uyainah that he said:

"Whoever's sin was because of [carnal] desires, hope for him (as he may repent and be forgiven); but whoever's sin was out of pride, fear for him. For indeed, Âdam sinned out of simple desire, and was forgiven; whereas Iblîs sinned out of pride, and was cursed."

Al-Dhahabî , Siyar A'lâm Al-Nubalâ` in his biography of Sufyân bin 'Uyainah.

'Abdullâh bin Mubârak said:

I asked Sufyân Al-Thawrî, "*When a man stands to pray, what should he intend by his recitation and prayer?*" He replied, "*He should intend that he is personally entreating his Lord.*"

Mu<u>h</u>ammad bin Na<u>s</u>r Al-Marwazî, Ta'<u>dh</u>îm Qadr Al-<u>S</u>alâh Vol. 1 p199.

Muʿādh bin Jabal used to say:

"Ahead of you are times of trials (fitan) in which there will be much wealth and in which the Qurān will be opened and taken (read) by believers and hypocrites, men and women, young and old and freemen and slaves. At that time it is likely that there will be people who will say, "Why aren't the people following me when I have read the Qurān? They will not follow me until I invent something else." So, beware of everything that is innovated (in religion), for those things that are innovated are misguidance."

Ibn Waḍḍāḥ, Al-Bidaʿ p62, Al-Lālakāʾī, Sharḥ Uṣūl Iʿtiqād Ahl Al-Sunnah wa Al-Jamāʿah 1:125, and others.

It is reported from 'Ubayd bin 'Umayr that he said:

"It used to be said when winter came: O people of the Qur`ân, the night has become long so you can pray (more) and the day has become short for you to fast."

Abû Nu'aym, Hilyah Al-Awliyâ`.

It is reported from the famous worshipper Râbi'ah that she said:

"I have never heard the adhân except that I remember the caller who will announce the Day of Resurrection, and I never see the falling snow except that I imagine the flying pages of the records of peoples deeds (on that day), and I never see swarms of locusts except that I think about the Great Gathering on the Last Day."

Ibn Al-Jawzî, Sifah Al-Safwah Vol. 2 p433.

Imâm Ahmad said:

"{Voluntary] bachelorhood has nothing to do with Islâm. The Prophet married fourteen women, and he died being married to nine of them. If Bishr bin Al-Hârith had married, his affairs would be complete. If people left marrying no one would go to battle or go on pilgrimage (Al-Hajj), and such-and-such wouldn't happen."

He went on to say:

"The Prophet would wake in the morning and his family would have nothing to eat and go to bed at night and they would have nothing to eat, [yet] he died married to nine wives, he chose marriage and encouraged others to marry."

Abû Bakr Al-Marrûdhî, Kitâb Al-Wara' p116, 117.

Ibn Mas'ūd used to say the takbīr during the Days of Tashrīq thus:

اللهُ أَكْبَرُ اللهُ أَكْبَر، لا إِلَهَ إِلاَّ الله

اللهُ أَكْبَرُ اللهُ أَكْبَر، وَ لِلهِ الحَمْد

Allāh is Greatest, Allāh is Greatest, none deserves worship but Allāh. Allāh is Greatest, Allāh is Greatest, and to Him is all praise.

Ibn Abī Shaybah, Al-Muṣannaf Vol.2 p74. Shaykh Al-Albānī said its chain of narration is Ṣaḥīḥ.

'Alī used to say the takbīr following the Fajr prayer on the Day of 'Arafah until the 'Aṣr prayer of the last day of Tashrīq – he used to say it after 'Aṣr prayer (then stop).

Ibn Abī Shaybah, Al-Muṣannaf Vol.2 p72. Shaykh Al-Albānī said its chain of narration is good.

See Irwā Al-Ghalīl Vol.3 p125.

It is reported from 'Abdullāh bin Mas'ūd that he said:

"*One should get used to the idea that if everyone on Earth disbelieved, you would not disbelieve. Do not be an im'ah (characterless*)."

He was asked, "*And what is an im'ah?*"

He replied, *"A person who says, 'I am with the people (I do what they do).' Verily, there is to be no following examples in evil."*

Ibn Ba<u>tt</u>ah, Al-Ibānah Al-Kubrā Vol.1 p33.

Some narrations reported from the Salaf in explanation of what it means to protect oneself and one's family as mentioned in Al-Tahrīm verse 6:

O you who believe! Protect yourselves and your families against a Fire (Hell) whose fuel is men and stones, over which are (appointed) angels, stern and severe, and who disobey not the commands they receive from Allāh, but do that which they are commanded. [66:6]

· 'Alī bin Abī Ṭālib said:

Discipline them, teach them.

· Ibn 'Abbās said:

Stay obedient to Allāh, stay away from disobeying Allāh and command your families to remember Allāh, and He will save you from the Fire.

· Mujāhid said:

Fear Allāh and obey him (practice taqwā) and tell your families to practice taqwā.

· Qatādah said:

A person protects his family by telling them to obey Allāh and forbidding them from disobeying Him. He upholds Allāh's commandments and helps his family to uphold them. So if you see some disobedience of Allāh you stop them from doing it, and you reprimand them.

Al-Ṭabarī, Al-Tafsīr, Sūrah Al-Taḥrīm.

It is reported from Al-Awzāʿī that he said:

"Whoever remembers death often will find a small amount (of worldly things) sufficient for him; and whoever includes his speech in his deeds will speak little."

Al-Dhahabī , Siyar A'lām Al-Nubalā` in his biography of Al-Awzāʿī.

It is reported from Al-Awzāʿī that he said:

"Knowledge is what has come from the Companions of Allah's Messenger; and what has not come from them is not knowledge."

Al-Dhahabī , Siyar A'lām Al-Nubalā` in his biography of Al-Awzāʿī. Ibn 'Asākir, Tārīkh Dimishq Vol.35 p201.

It is reported from ʿAbdullah bin Mas'ūd that he said:

"For every bid'ah with which Islām is plotted against, Allah has a beloved worshipper (walī) who refutes and repels it and speaks about its signs, so take the full opportunity of attending such places, and trust in Allah."

Ibn Wa<u>dd</u>āḥ, Al-Bid'ah p5.

'Alī bin Abī Ṭālib said:

"Narrate to people what they can understand; do you want Allah and His Messenger to be disbelieved?"

Quoted by Al-Bukhārī, Al-Ṣaḥīḥ, Chapter about a person preferring some people with certain knowledge to the exclusion of others.

Ibn Ḥajr said in Fatḥ Al-Bārī, *"[In this narration] there is evidence that ambiguous knowledge should not be mentioned amongst the general public."*

Shaykh Muḥammad bin Ṣāliḥ Al-'Uthaymīn explained this very important and often misunderstood point beautifully. After mentioning the narration of 'Alī, he states:

It is therefore an aspect of wisdom in da'wah (calling others to Allah) that you should not surprise people with things they are not able to comprehend. Rather, you should call them in stages, bit by bit until their minds settle..."

He goes on to say:

"[The statement of 'Alī] '*Do you want Allah and His Messenger to be disbelieved?' is a rhetorical question, posed as a criticism of such behavior. It means: by narrating to people things they cannot understand do you want Allah and His Messenger to be disbelieved? This is because in such cases when you say, "Allah said, and His Messenger said" they will say you have lied if their minds cannot comprehend what you are saying. Here, they are not disbelieving Allah and His Messenger, but they are disbelieving you because of this speech that you have attributed to Allah and His Messenger. Thus they will end up disbelieving Allah and His Messenger – not directly – but by way of the one who transmits this knowledge (i.e. you).*

Now if it is said: Should we stop telling people things they cannot understand even if they need to know? The answer is: no, we do not leave this knowledge altogether, but we should tell them in a way that they will be able to understand. This is done by telling them stage by stage, bit by bit until they can accept the speech we want them to know and they can feel comfortable with it. We do not abandon knowledge that people cannot understand and just say 'this is something they will reject or dislike so we will not speak about it.'

The same is the case with acting upon a Sunnah that people are not used to and which they might find objectionable. We should act by this Sunnah, but only after informing people about it, such that they will be able to accept it and feel comfortable about it.

We learn from this narration (of 'Alī) that it is important to employ wisdom in calling to Allah, and that it is incumbent upon anyone who calls to Allah to consider the level of understanding of those he is inviting, and that he should put everyone in their proper place.

Majmū' Fatāwā Ibn 'Uthaymīn Vol.10 p140.

Al-Qāsim bin Muhammad, grandson of Abū Bakr said:

"In my time the people were not impressed by speech, they were impressed by actions. Anyone can say whatever he wants."

Abū Dāwūd, Kitāb Al-Zuhd p354.

Hasan al Basri said:

"There is no backbiting for a person of innovation or a person who openly commits sins."

Al-Laalikaa'ee in Sharh-Usoolul-I'tiqaad 1/140

Ibn Abī Mulaykah said:

"I met thirty of the Prophet's Companions – Allah's peace and blessings be upon him – and every one of them feared falling into nifāq (hypocrisy); not one of them claimed he had the level of faith of Jibrīl or Mīkā'īl."

Quoted by Al-Bukhārī, Al-S̲ah̲īh̲, Chapter on the believer fearing that his deeds will be nullified without him realizing.

ʿAbdullāh bin Mas'ūd went to visit someone who was ill, and a group of people went with him. In the house (where they were visiting) was a woman. One of the visitors, a man, started to look at the woman. ʿAbdullāh said to him, *"If your eye had been gouged out (or popped out] it would have been better for you."*

Al-Bukhārī, Al-Adab Al-Mufrad. See Shaykh Al-Albānī's S̲ah̲īh̲ Al-Adab Al-Mufrad Vol.1 p212.

Abū Hurayrah said:

"There is no illness that afflicts me more beloved to me than fever: it enters every part of me and [because of it] Allah the Mighty and Sublime gives every part of me its share of reward."

Al-Bukhārī, Al-Adab Al-Mufrad. See Shaykh Al-Albānī's S̲ah̲īh̲ Al-Adab Al-Mufrad Vol.1 p198.

It is reported from 'Alī bin Abī T̲ālib that he said:

"The thing I fear for you most is following desires and having extensive hopes (about this worldly life). Following one's desires blocks you from the truth, and having extensive hopes makes you forget the hereafter. Verily, this worldly life is departing and the hereafter is approaching and each of them has its children. So be children of the hereafter, not children of this world, for today

there are (opportunities to do) deeds and there is no reckoning, but tomorrow there will be reckoning and no deeds."

Reported by Abū Nu'aym, H̲ilyah Al-Awliyā` Vol.1 p40, and others.

Al-H̲āfidh Ibn H̲ajr states in Fath̲ Al-Bārī:

"Extensive hopes (about this worldly life) give rise to lethargy when it comes to acts of obedience, procrastinating with repentance, desire for worldly things, forgetfulness of the hereafter and hardness of the heart; because the softness of the heart and its purity only comes about by remembering death, the grave, reward and punishment, and the horrors of the hereafter...for if one remembers death, he strives to do acts of obedience, his worries decrease and he is satisfied with less."

Whenever asked about a matter, Zayd bin Thābit would himself ask, "*Has this happened?*" If they told him that the matter had not yet occurred he would not inform them of an answer, but if they told him it had happened he would answer them.

Al-Ājurrī, Akhlāq Al-'Ulamā` no.81; Al-Khat̲īb, Al-Faqīh wa Al-Mutafaqqih Vol2. P13.

Abū 'Umar Al-Shaybānī reports:

I would sit with Ibn Mas'ūd a whole year without him saying "Allah's Messenger said..." When he did actually say "Allah's Messenger said..." he would tremble and add, "...or something similar to this" or "words to that effect."

Al-Dhahabī, Tadhkirah Al-H̲uffādh Vol.1 p15.

Sufyān bin 'Uyainah said:

"The first step in knowledge is to listen, then to be quiet and attentive, then to preserve it, then to put it into practice and then to spread it."

Abū Nu'aym, Hilyah Al-Awliyā` Vol.3 p283.

A man came to Maymūn bin Mahrānto ask for his daughter's hand in marriage. Maymūn said, "*I do not approve of her for you.*" The man asked, "*Why?*" He replied, "*Because she loves jewelry and garments.*" To this the man said, "*Well I have as much of those as she desires.*" Maymūn said, "*Now I don't approve of you for her.*"

Al-Dhahabī , Siyar A'lām Al-Nubalā` in his biography of Maymūn bin Mahrān.

It is reported from Maymūn bin Mahrān that he said:

"A person cannot be a taqīy (pious man of taqwā) until he takes account of himself like he would with his business partner; and until he knows where he gets his clothing and food and drink."

Wakī' bin Al-Jarrāh, Al-Zuhd Vol.1 p270.

It is reported from Sufyān Al-Thawrī that he said:

"A person who sits with a heretic (an adherent of bid'ah) will not escape one of three things:Either he will become a trial (fitnah) for others, or some deviation will occur in his heart and he will slip and be cast into the Fire by Allah, or he will say to himself, 'By Allah, I don't care what they say, I am confident about myself;' but whoever feels secure from Allah about his religion

even for the blinking of an eye, Allah will take his religion away from him."

Ibn Waddāḥ, Al-Bida' p125.

Al-Hasan Al-Basrī said:

"Do not sit with an adherent of bid'ah for he will cause a disease in your heart."

Ibn Waddāh, Al-Bida' p124.

It is reported Abū Idrīs Al-Khawlānī used to say:

"I would rather hear of a fire in the masjid than hear of a bid'ah in it without there being anyone to do away with it. Never do a people innovate a bid'ah in their religion except that Allah removes a sunnah from them."

Ibn Waddāh, Al-Bida' p92.

Al-Hasan Al-Basrī said:

"When a man sought knowledge, it would not be long before it could be seen in his humbleness, his sight, upon his tongue and his hands, in his prayer, in his speech and in his disinterest (zuhd) in worldly allurements. And a man would acquire a portion of knowledge and put it into practice, and it would be better for him than the world and all it contains if he owned it he would give it in exchange for the hereafter."

Ibn Al-Mubārak, Al-Zuhd wa Al-Raqā`iq Vol.1 p.156.

'Abdullah bin Mas'ūd said:

"Everyone speaks of good things. It is those whose words and deeds match who have acquired their share. Those whose words and deeds do not match have only reproached themselves."

Ibn Al-Mubārak, Al-Zuhd wa Al-Raqā`iq Vol.1 p.153.

Bilāl bin Sa'd said:

"Do not think about how small the sin is, but think about who you have just disobeyed."

Ibn Al-Mubārak, Al-Zuhd wa Al-Raqā`iq Vol.1 p150.

It is reported that before his death, Abū Mūsā Al-Ash'arī used to exert himself intensely in worship. It was said to him, *"If only you would slow down and go easy on yourself."* He replied, *"When steeds are let loose and come close to the end of their course they finish by giving it all they have, and what remains of my life is less than that."*

Al-Dhahabī , Siyar A'lām Al-Nubalā` in his biography of Abū Mūsā Al-Ash'arī.

'Abdullah bin Mas'ūd said:

"Singing sprouts hypocrisy (nifāq) in the heart as water sprouts greens and herbs."

Ibn Battah, Al-Ibānah Al-Kubrā Vol.2 p469, and Al-Bayhaqī, Al-Sunan Al-Kubrā Vol. 52 p231.

A man once asked Muhammad bin Wāsi' for advice. He replied, *"I advise you to be a king in this world and the hereafter."* The man enquired, "How?" He replied, *"Lose interest in worldly things (practice zuhd)."*

Al-Dhahabī , Siyar A'lām Al-Nubalā` in his biography of Mu<u>h</u>ammad bin Wāsi'.

Mu<u>h</u>ammad bin Wāsi' said:

"I have lived amongst men who were such that one of them would lie with his wife on the same pillow and his side of the pillow would be soaked with his tears under his cheek without his wife even noticing."

Ibn Abī Al-Dunyā, Al-Ikhlā<u>s</u> wa Al-Nīyah (Sincerity and Intentions) p34.

Imām Ibrāhīm Al-Nakha'ī said about the Salaf:

"When in a gathering, they used to dislike a person showing the best of what he has."

Ibn Abī Al-Dunyā, Al-Ikhlā<u>s</u> wa Al-Nīyah (Sincerity and Intentions) p50.

Explanation of the verse:

Nay, but their hearts were covered over by what (sins) they earned. [Al-Mu<u>t</u>affifīn: 14]

Al-Hasan (Al-Ba<u>s</u>rī) said, *"It is because of doing one sin after another, until the heart becomes blind and dies."*

Qatādah also said, *"It is because of doing one sin after another, one sin after another, until the heart dies and becomes black."*

Ibn Zayd said, *"Their sins overcome their hearts until no good can get through to them."*

Mujāhid explained, *"They used to consider the heart like a hand: when a person sins, his heart starts to scrunch up,"* and he folded his little finger, "*and when he does another sin,*" he folded the next finger and continued until he had his fist clenched. "*Then a seal is placed over it, and they used to say that this is the 'covering'.*"

Al-Ṯabarī in his Tafsīr, Sūrah Al-Muṯaffifīn.

It is reported from Abū Al-'Āliyah that he said:

"A fasting person is in a state of worship as long as he does not backbite, even if he is sleeping in bed."

Al-Imām Aẖmad, Al-Zuhd Vol.4 p313.

ʿAbdullah bin Mas'ūd said:

"The believer sees his sins as if he is sitting at the foot of a mountain fearing that it might fall on him, while the sinner (fājir) sees his sins as a fly that lands on his nose, he just waves it away."

Al-Bukhārī, Al-S̲ah̲īh̲, The Book of Supplications, Chapter on Tawbah.

ʿAbdullah Ibn 'Abbās was asked, "*Who do you think is better: a man who has few (good) deeds and few sins or a man who has many (good) deeds and many sins?*" He replied, "*There is nothing like being safe.*"

Ibn Al-Mubārak, Al-Zuhd wa Al-Raqā`iq Vol.1 p146, no.57.

ʿAbd Al-Raḥmān bin Abī Laylā said:

"I have met one hundred and twenty Companions of the Prophet; there was not one amongst them who would narrate a ḥadīth except that he wished his brother would suffice him instead, and

there was not one amongst them who gave a fatwā except that he wished his brother would suffice him instead."

Ibn Al-Mubārak, Al-Zuhd wa Al-Raqā`iq Vol.1 p140, no.49.

It is reported from 'Ā`ishah that she said:

"You will never meet Allah with anything better for you than having few sins. Whoever wants to surpass those who exert themselves in worship, let him stop himself from committing numerous sins."

Ibn Al-Jawzī, Sifah Al-Safwah Vol.1 p319.

It is reported that 'Umar bin Al-Khattāb said:

"Do not be fooled by one who recites the Qurān. His recitation is but speech – but look to those who act according to it."

Al-Khatīb, Iqtidā` Al-'Ilm Al-'Amal no. 109

It is reported from Ayyūb Al-Sakhtiyānī [d130H] that he said:

"There is no filth filthier than the sinful (fājir) reciter of the Qurān."

Al-Khatīb, Iqtidā` Al-'Ilm Al-'Amal no. 114

It is reported from Al-Fudayl (bin 'Ayyāḍ) that he said:

"The Qurān was sent down to be acted upon but people have taken just reciting it as enough of a deed." He was asked, "How is it acted upon?" He replied, "They should treat as halāl what it makes halāl and treat as harām what it makes harām, they should take on its commandments and stay away from what it forbids, and they should stop to ponder its amazing knowledge and wisdom."

Al-Khaṯīb, Iqtiḏā` Al-'Ilm Al-'Amal no. 116

Imām Mālik said: "

Knowledge is not to be taken from four types of people: a foolish person who openly acts foolish, even if he reports the most narrations; an adherent of bid'ah who calls to his desires; a person who lies, even if I don't accuse him of lying in ḥadīth; and a righteous pious worshipper who does not accurately retain what he narrates."

Al-Dhahabī , Siyar A'lām Al-Nubalā` in his biography of Imām Mālik.

'Abdullah bin Zayd Al-Numayrī reports that Al-Ḥasan Al-Baṣrī said:

"They (the heretics) were destroyed by their inability in Arabic (al-'ujmah)."

Al-Bukhārī, Al-Tārīkh Al-Kabīr Vol.5 p99.

Al-Fuḏayl bin 'Ayyāḍ said:

"Allah accepts only those deeds which are both correct and sincere (pure). If the deed is done correctly but not sincerely, it will not be accepted. And if it is sincere but not correct, it will not be accepted." He was asked, "Abū 'Alī! What is the sincere and correct deed?" He replied, "The sincere deed is one that is done only for Allah. And the correct deed is one done according to the Sunnah."

Abū Nu'aym, H̲ilyah Al-Awliyā` Vol.8 p95.

Yūsuf bin Asbāṯ reports that whenever Sufyān remembered the hereafter he would urinate blood.

It is also reported that Sufyān said:

"I sometimes see something I feel I am obliged to speak out about, but when I don't say anything I urinate blood."

And in another report:

"I sometimes see an evil being done, but if I don't speak out about it I urinate blood."

Al-Dhahabī , Siyar A'lām Al-Nubalā` in his biography of Imām Sufyān Al-Thawrī .

Abū Ibrāhīm Al-Muzanī, the companion of Imām Al-Shāfi'ī reports:

I heard Al-Shāfi'ī comment on the statement of Allah:

Nay, they (the unbelievers) will be on that day veiled from their Lord. [Al-Muṭaffifīn: 15]

He said, *"In this verse there is evidence that the awliyā` of Allah (His beloved righteous worshippers) will see their Lord on the Day of Resurrection."*

Al-Lālakā`ī in Sharḥ Usūl I'tiqād Ahl Al-Sunnah wa Al-Jamā'ah Vol.2 p309.

Ibrāhīm bin ʿAbd Al-Raḥmān bin 'Auf reports:

ʿUmar bin Al-Khaṯṯāb was given the treasures of the Persian Emperor (after his conquest), ʿAbdullah bin Arqam asked, *"Are you going to put this into the public treasury (bayt al-māl) until you can distribute it?"* ʿUmar replied, *"No by Allah, I will not take this under a roof before I have passed it on."* So they put it in the middle of the mosque and spent the night guarding it. In the morning, ʿUmar uncovered the treasure and saw such an amount of gold and silver that it almost shone; so he began to cry. ʿAbd Al-Raḥmān bin ʿAuf said, "*Why do you cry o Amīr of the Believers? This is a day of thanks and a day of happiness for sure.*" ʿUmar replied, "*Woe to you, this has never been given to a people except that it has cast enmity and hatred amongst them.*"

Ibn Al-Mubārak in Al-Zuhd wa Al-Raqā`iq Vol. 2 p595, 596.

Masrūq said:

"Sufficient as knowledge for a person is that he fears Allah, and sufficient as ignorance for a person is that he feels impressed with the knowledge he has."

Al-Ājurrī in Akhlāq Al-'Ulamā' no.40.

Masrūq was one of the major Tābi'īn, or students of the Companions. He accompanied Ibn Mas'ūd and was one of his students who became senior teachers and muftis after him. He reported from numerous other S̲ah̲ābah. It is said that he was called Masrūq (literally: stolen) because he was kidnapped as a child but later recovered. He died in 62H or 63H.

Sulaymān bin Mūsā [d119H] said:

"When you fast, your hearing and sight should also fast, and your tongue should fast by keeping away from lies; and do not harm your servant. Don't let the day you fast be the same as the day you don't fast."

Tārīkh Dimishq Vol. 22 p389.

Al-S̲awm (fasting) literally means to keep away from something. Fasting of the faculties of hearing and seeing means to keep away from listening to and looking at things that are displeasing to Allah, in the same way that we stay away from food and drink when we are fasting.

'Ikrimah, Sumay' and Kurayb report that Ibn 'Abbās said to them:

"Marry, for if the servant of Allah commits fornication Allah snatches the light of īmān from him, and may or may not return it to him."

Ibn Sa'd in Al-Ṭabaqāt Al-Kubra Vol.5 p287.

It is reported that there used to be poor people in Al-Madīnah who didn't know where they were getting their food from. When 'Alī bin Ḥusayn passed away, they started missing what they used to be given at night.

Abū Ḥamzah Al-Thumālī narrates that 'Alī bin Ḥusayn used to carry bread on his back in the darkness of the night and follow the poor people (to give it to them). He used to say, *"Charity in the darkness of the night extinguishes the Lords anger."*

'Amr bin Thābit reports that when 'Alī bin Ḥusayn died, they found marks on his back from the sacks of provisions he used to carry at night to the houses of the widows.

Shaybah bin Nu'āmah narrates that when 'Alī bin Ḥusayn died they found out that he used to provide for a hundred (poor) families.

Al-Dhahabī in Siyar A'lām Al-Nubalā' under the biography of 'Alī bin Ḥusayn Zayn Al-'Ābidīn.

A fire once broke out in a house where 'Alī bin Husayn was prostrate in prayer. He didn't raise his head until the fire went out. When asked about this he said:

"The other Fire kept my mind busy."

Al-Dhahabī in Siyar A'lām Al-Nubalā' under the biography of 'Alī bin Husayn Zayn Al-'Ābidīn.

Abū Al-Dardā' said:

"It is from a person's knowledge and understanding that he sees to his needs first in order to turn to his prayer with a heart free of distractions."

Ibn Al-Mubārak in Al-Zuhd wa Al-Raqā'iq Vol.2 p726

Imām Al-Shāfi'ī said:

"Whenever any people of desires (heretics) came to Mālik he would say to them, "As for me, I am upon clarity as regards my religion. As for you, you are a doubter, go and argue with another doubter like yourself.""

Al-Dhahbī in Siyar A'lām Al-Nubalā' under the biography of Imām Mālik.

Al-Hārith bin Qays said:

"When intending to do something good, do not delay it until tomorrow. When involved in something to do with the hereafter, keep yourself involved as long as you can. When involved in some worldly matter, put your mind to it. And if you are praying and Shaytān whispers, 'You are showing off,' then make your prayer even longer."

Ibn Al-Mubārak in Al Zuhd wa Al-Rqā'iq Vol.1 p126

Abu Al-'Āliyah reports that a man once asked 'Ubay bin Ka'b for advice. He said:

"Take the Book of Allah as your leader (imām) and be pleased with it as a judge and ruler. It is what your Messenger left amongst you. It will be an intercessor for you. It is to be obeyed. It is a witness never doubted. In it is a mention of you and those before you, and judgment for whatever happens amongst you. And in it is news about you and whatever will come after you."

Al-Dhahabī in Siyar A'lām Al-Nubalā', in the biography of 'Ubay bin Ka'b

'Aṭā' narrates that there used to be a young man who used to go to Mother of the Believers 'Ā'ishah to ask her questions and she would narrate to him. One day, he came to her to ask her some questions. She said, "*Son, have you put into practice what you hear from me yet?*" He replied, "*No mother, I have not.*" So she said, "*Son, why do you then seek to increase Allah's proof against us and you?!*"

Al-Khatīb Al-Baghdādī in Iqtidā' Al-'Ilm Al-'Amal no. 92.

A man once asked Ka'b, "Which illness cannot be treated?" "Death", he replied.

The son of Zayd bin Aslam said:

My father said, "*There is one treatment for death: gaining the pleasure of Allah.*"

Ibn Abī Al-Dunyā in Dhikr Al-Mawt no. 418.

Al-Ḥasan Al-Baṣrī said:

"Faith (īmān) is not by embellishment or wishful thinking, but it is what settles in the heart and is verified through your works. Whoever says good but does not do good will have his words compared to his deeds by Allah. Whoever says good and does good will have his words raised by his deeds. This is because Allah said:

To Him ascends the good word, and the righteous deed raises it. [Sūrah Fāṭir: 10]"

Ibn Ba<u>tt</u>ah in Al-Ibānah Al-Kubrā Vol. 3 p120, and Al-Khaṭīb Al-Baghdādī in Iqtiḍā' Al-'Ilm Al-'Amal no.56.

Ma'n bin 'Īsa Al-Qazzāz reports:

Whenever Mālik bin Anas would sit to narrate ḥadīth he would bath and perfume himself. If anyone raised his voice in the gathering [Imām Mālik] would reprimand him and say, *"Lower your voice, for Allah tabāraka wa ta'ālā said:*

O Believers! Do not raise your voices over that of the Prophet [Sūrah Al-Ḥujarāt: 2]

Whoever raises his voice over the sound of the ḥadīth of Allah's Messenger, then it is as if he is raising his voice over that of the Prophet."

Na<u>s</u>r bin Ibrāhīm Al-Maqdisī in Mukhta<u>s</u>ar Al-<u>H</u>ujjah 'alā Tārik Al-Ma<u>h</u>ajjah Vol.1 p121.

Abū 'Uthmān Sa'īd bin Ismā'īl Al-Naysābūrī said:

"Whoever governs himself by the Sunnah – in word and deed – will speak with wisdom. But whoever governs himself according

to his own desires will speak heresies (bid'ah); because Allah said:

And if you obey him (the Messenger) you will be guided. [Sūrah Al-Nūr: 54]"

Abū Nu'aym in Al-Ḥilyah Vol.10 p244, and others.

After mentioning this and other similar narrations Shaykh Al-Islām Ibn Taymīyah said (Minhāj Al-Sunnah Vol.5 p117):

It is as they said, for if a person does not follow what the Messenger came with he will act according to his own wishes. Thus he will be one who follows his desires without guidance from Allah.

A man once asked Abū Al-Dardā' for advice. He said:

"Remember Allāh in good times and He will mention you in hard times. When you remember those who have passed away, consider yourself like one of them. And when you think of involving yourself in some worldly matter, consider first what it will lead to in the end."

Al-Dhahabī in Siyar A'lām Al-Nubalā', under the biography of Abū Al-Dardā'.

'Abdullah bin 'Umar said:

"Every bid'ah (religious innovation) is misguidance, even if people think it is good."

Al-Lālakā'ī in Sharh Usūl I'tiqād Ahl Al-Sunnah wa Al-Jamā'ah Vol 1. P134, no.111; and Ibn Baṯṯah in Al-Ibānah Al-Kubraa Vol.1 p219, no. 213

Anas bin Mālik said:

"You people do things today that you regard as less significant than a strand of hair, whereas we, during the time of the Prophet used to consider them destructive sins."

Al-Bukhārī in his Ṣaḥīḥ, Chapter on sins that are seen as insignificant but which should be kept away from.

Commenting on 2:201 of the Quran which states:

Our Lord! Give us the good of this world and the good of the hereafter...

Al-Hasan Al-Baṣrī said:

"The good of this world is knowledge and worship, and the good of the hereafter is Paradise."

Al-Ājurrī in Akhlāq Al-'Ulamā' no. 30 and Ibn Jarīr in his Tafsīr of this verse.

'Alī bin Abī Ṭālib said:

"Shall I not tell you who the real faqīh is? He is one who does not make people despair of Allah's mercy, yet he does not give them concessions to disobey Allah. He does not make them feel safe from Allah's plan and he does not leave the Quran.

There is no good in worship that involves no efforts to gain fiqh, and there is no good in seeking fiqh without seeking a thorough understanding. And there is no good in reading without contemplating."

Al-Ājurrī in Akhlāq Al-'Ulamā' no. 45, Al-Khaṭīb in Al-Faqīh wa Al-Mutafaqqih Vol. 2 pp338-339.

Imam Adh-Dhahabee said:

"May Allah have mercy over the person who speaks little, reads the Quran, weeps over his lost time, constanty gazes into (saheeh) Bukharee and (saheeh) Muslim, and worships Allah before he is surprised by death."

At-Tadhkirah, 2/80

Sufyaan ibn Uyaynah said:

"The Sunnah is ten things, whosoever accepts them has completed the Sunnah, and whosoever abandons anything from them has abandoned the Sunnah...(and the last one he mentioned was) and not testifying that any Muslim will definitely be in Paradise or Hell (except with a textual proof)."

Al-Laalakaa'ee, no 312

Imam Ahmad said:

"The companions of the Messenger of Allah-after the four caliphs-are the best of the people, and it is not permissible for anyone to speak ill of any of them, blaming them for deficiencies and shortcomingsl It is indeed obligatory upon the ruler to reprimand and punish whoever does that, and he should not be pardoned."

Kitaab As-Sunnah p. 77-78 & Manaaqibul Imam Ahmad, of Ibnul Jawzee p. 170

Imam Malik said:

"The shield of the Scholar is "I do not know", so if he leaves it down, his attacker will strike him."

Al-Intiqaa p.37

Ibn Adbil-Barr said:

"It is authentically related from Abu Dardaa that "I do not know" is half of knowledge."

Jaami Bayaanil Ilm Wa Fadhlih 1/54

Muaadh ibn Jabal said:

"O people, you must seek knowledge before it is taken away, for indeed when its people (the scholars) die, it will be taken away. And beware of bidah, innovation and sophistication and adhere to the ancient way (the way of the Prophet)."

Al-Bidaayah Wannahy'anha by Ibn Waddaah

Abu Bakr bin Abdullah al Muzani said:

"Who is like you, O son of Adam? Whenever you wish, you use water to make ablution, go to the place for worship and thus enter the presence of your Lord (start praying) without a translator/barrier or a barrier between you and Him!"

Al Bidayah Wan-Nihayah 9/256

Huhayfah bin Al-Yamaan said:

"Do not perform any act of worship that was not practiced by the Companions of the Messenger of Allah, for the earlier generation did not leave any room for the latter to add anything(to the religion). Fear Allah, O readers, seekers of knowledge, and follow the path of those who came before you."

Narrated by Ibn Battah in Al-Ibaanah

Ibn Shubrumah said:

"I am amazed at the people who take care of themselves by eating food out of fear of dying, yet do not protect themselves from sins out of fear of the Fire."

Siyar A'laam an Nubalaa 6/348

Imam Ahmad ibn Hanbal said:

"Describe Allah with what He has described Himself with, and negate from Allah what He has negated from Himself"

Manaaqibul Imam Ahmad by Ibn Al Jawzee p. 221

Imam Ahmad bin Hanbal also said:

"and in no way is Allah to be described with anything more than what He-the Mighty and Majestic-has described himself with."

Kitaabul-Mhnah p.68

Abdullah ibn Masood said:

"Whoever wants to follow an example, let him follow the example of those who have passed away, the Companions of Muhammad. They were the best of this ummah, the purest in heart, the deepest in knowledge, the least in sophistication. They were people whom Allah chose to be the Companions of his Prophet and to convey His religion, so imitate their ways and behavior, for they were following the Straight Path."

Al Baghawi in Sharh as Sunnah

Haytham ibn Jameel was asked:

"A man is well learned with regards to the affairs of the Sunnah, should he debate and argue about them?"

He replied:

"No, however he should inform the people about the Sunnah, so if it is accepted from him then good and if not then he should keep silent."

Jaami'u Bayaan Al-Ilmi Wa Fadhlihi, 4/94

Imam Ahmad said:

"Whosoever alleges that Allah does not speak, then he is a disbeliever. Verily we relay these narrations as they have come."

As-Sunnah p. 71

Abdullah ibn Masood said:

"Follow and do not innovate, for everything has been taken care of and you must follow the ancient way (of the salaf)."

Ad-Daarimi in his Sunan

Sufyaan Ath-Thawri said:

"The excellence of knowledge is due only to the fact that it causes a person to fear and obey Allah, otherwise it is just like anything else."

Related by Ibn Rajab

Al Hasan al Basri said:

"Whoever learns something in the name of Allah, seeking that which is with Him, he will win. And whoever learns something for other than Allah, he will not reach the goal, nor will his acquired knowledge bring him closer to Allah."

Related by ibn ul Jawzee

Abdullah ibn Masood said:

"The Jamaah is whatever agrees with the truth-even if you are alone."

Reported in Taarekh Dimashq with an authentic chain of narration

Ishaaq ibn Raahawaih (d. 238H), (the teacher of Imam Bukhari) said:

"If you were to ask the ignorant people about the "Main Body" they would say, "The majority of people" they do not know that the jamaa'ah is the scholar who clings to the narrations from the Prophet and his way. So whoever is with him(the scholar) and follows him, then he is the Jamaah."

Abu Nuaym in Hilyatul Awliyaah

Abdullah ibn Umar said:

"Every bidah is misguidance, even if people think it is good."

Al-Laalkaa'I in Sharh Usool Itiqaad Ahl as Sunnah wal Jamaah

Shaqeeq al Balkhee said:

"The sign of repentence (is) weeping at what has preceded, fear of falling into sin, leaving evil company and maintaining the company of the good."

Siyar A'laam an Nubalaa, 9/315

Abu ad-Darda said:

"You will never be misguided so long as you follow the footsteps[of the Prophet]."

Ibn Battah in Al-Ibaanah

Yahya ibn Maeen said:

"Defending the Sunnah is more excellent than Jihad in Allah's cause." So it was said to Yahya ibn Maeen,"A man spends his wealth, tires himself out and fights in Jihad, and this one(who defends the sunnah) is more excellent than him?" He said: "Yes, by a great deal"

Siyaar Alaamin Nubulaa of Adh Dhahabee Vol. 10 p. 512-519

Abdullah ibn Masood said:

"Study and act upon what you learn."

Related by Abu Naeem

Abdullah ibn Amr ibn al-Aas said:

"No bidah is introduced but it will spread further and no Sunnah is neglected but it will diminish further."

Ibn Battah in Al Ibaanah

Talq ibn Habeeb said:

"Indeed the rights of Allah are far greater than the servant can fulfill, and indeed the blessings of Allah are far more than can be counted, however, be repentul in the morning and evening.

Siyar Alaam an-Nubalaa 4/622

Imam Al Awzaai said:

"You must follow the footsteps of those who came before, even if the people reject you. Beware of personal opinions even if people make them attractive. The clear way is that of the Straight Path."

Al Khateeb in Sharaf Ashaab al-Hadith

Ayyaoob as-Sakhtiyaani said:

"The more the innovator increases his efforts in innovation, the further away he becomes from Allah."

Al Biah Wan-Nahy'anha by Ibn Waddaah

Hassan ibn Atiyah said:

"No people introduce innovation into their religion but an equivalent amount of Sunnah will be taken away."

Al-Laalkaa'I in Sharh Usool I'tiqaad Ahl as-sunnah wal-Jamaah

Ibn Abbaas said:

"Indeed the most detestable of things to Allah are the innovations."

As-Sunan al Kubraa 4/316

Sufyaan Ath-Thawri said:

"Innovation is more beloved to Iblis than sin, since a sin may be repented from but innovation is not repented from."

Sharh Usool I'tiqaad Ahlis-Sunnah wal-Jamaah #238

Al Hasan al Basri said:

"Do not sit with the people of innovation and desires, nor argue with them, nor listen to them."

Sunan Ad-Daarimee, 1/121

Al-Fudayl ibn Iyaad said:

"I met the best of people, all of them people of the Sunnah and they used to forbid from accompanying people of innovation."

Sharh Usool I'tiqaad Ahlis Sunnah wal Jamaah, #267

Ibrahim ibn Maysarah said:

"Whoever honours an innovator has aided in the destruction of Islam."

Sharh Usool I'tiqaad Ahlis-Sunnah wal Jamaah 1/139

Sufyaan Ath-Thawri said:

"Whoever listens to an innovator has left the protection of Allah and is entrusted with the innovation."

Al-Hilyah, 7/26

Imam al Barbahaaree said:

"the innovators are like scorpions. They bury their heads and bodies in the sand and leave their tails out. When they get the chance they sting, the same with the innovators who conceal themselves amongst the people, when they are able, they do what they desire."

Tabaqaatul-Hanaabilah, 2/44

Abu Haatim said:

"A sign of the people of innovation is their battling against the people of Narrations."

As-Saffaareenee said:

"And we are not focusing on mentioning the virtues of the people of Hadith, for indeed their virtues are well known and their merits are many. So whoever belittles them, then he is despicable and lowly. And whoever hates them, then he is from the backwared party of the Devil."

Lawaa'ihul Anwaar, 2/355

Abu Uthman As-Saaboonee said:

"The signs of the people of innovation are clear and obvious. The most apparent of their signs is their severe enmity for those who carry the reports of the Prophet."

The Aqeedah of the (Pious) Predecessors p. 101

Muhammad ibn An-Nadr Al-Haarithee said:

"Whoever listens to a person of innovation-and knows that he is a person of innovation-then protection is taken away from him, and he is left to himself."

Sharh Usool I'tiqaad 1/135-136

Imam ash-Shaatibee mentioned:

"Linguistically bidah means "a newly invented matter". The Shariah definition of bidah as: "A newly invented way [beliefs or action] in the religion, in imitation of the Shariah, by which nearness to allah is sought, [but] not being supported by any authentic proof-neither in its foundations, nor in the manner in which it is performed."

Al-I'tisaam of ash-Shaatibee 1/37

Ali ibn abi Talib said:

"Verily knowledge is more precious than wealth. Knowledge preserves you, while you preserve wealth. Knowledge judges while wealth is judged upon. The possessors of wealth have died, while the possessors of knowledge live on. Their (the scholars) bodies have passed away, but they are still present in the hearts of the people."

Adab Al-Dunya wa Al-Deen p. 48

Malik bin Dinar said:

"The greatest punishment a slave (of Allah) can get is hard heartedness."

Narrated by Abdullah bin Ahmed in Kitab Al-Zuhd

Ar-Rabee ibn Sulaymaan said:

"One day Ash-Shaafi narrated a hadith, and a man said to him "Do you accept that O Abu Abdullah?" He said, "If I narrate a saheeh hadith from the Messenger of Allah and I do not accept it, then bear witness that I have lost my mind."

Ibn Battah in Al Ibaanah

Imam Ahmad said:

"If you see anyone speaking ill of the Companions of the Messenger of Allah, doubt his Islam."

Al-Laalikaa'ee in As-Sunnah, 2359

Imam Malik said:

"The Sunnah is like the ship of Nuh. Whoever rides in it will be saved and whoever hangs back and does not get on board will be drowned."

Miftaah al-Jannah fil-I'tisaam bis-Sunnah by As-Suyooti

Imam Ahmad ibn Hanbal said:

"The basic principles of Sunnah in our view are: adherence to the way of the Companions of the Messenger of Allah, following their example and forsaking bidah, for every bidah is a going astray."

Al-Laalkaa'I in Sharh Usool Ahl as-Sunnah

Imam Malik said:

"Truly I am only a mortal: I make mistakes (sometimes) and I am correct (sometimes). Therefore, look into my opinions: all that

agrees with the Book and the Sunnah, accept it, and all that does not agree with the Book and the Sunnah, ignore it."

Ibn Abdul Barr in Jaami Bayaan al Ilm 2/32

Imam Abu Hanifah said:

"When I say something contradicting the Book of Allah the Exalted or what is narrated from the Messenger, then ignore my saying."

Al-Fulaani in Eeqaaz Al Himam p. 50

Imam Ash-Shaafi said:

"The Muslims are unanimously agreed that if a sunnah of the Messenger of Allah is made clear to someone, it is not permitted for him to leave it for the saying of anyone else."

I'laam 2/361

Imam Ahmad said:

"Do not follow my opinion; neither follow the opinion of Malik, nor Shafi, nor Awzaai, nor Thawri, but take from where they took."

Ibn al Qayyim in I'laam 2/302

Sufyan bin Uyaynah said:

"Honoring the prayer includes coming before the Iqamah is recited."

Sifat as Safwah 2/235

Al Fudayl ibn Iyaad said:

"Follow the path of guidance, and do not worry about how few are the people who follow it. Beware of the paths of misguidance and do not be deceived by the large numbers of those who are doomed."

Al-I'tisaam by Imam Ash-Shaatibi

Abu Bakr said:

"Let not any Muslim belittle another Muslim, for the least of the Muslims is great in the Sight of Allah."

Ihya Ulum ad-din, 3/400

Muhammad bin al Husayn bin Ali said:

"The heart of a person is never afflicted with the slightest bit of arrogance except that his intelligence and sanity is decreased because of that in accordance with how much of that arrogance has entered his heart."

Ihya' Ulum ad-Din, 3/400

Abdul Qaadir Al-Jeelaanee said:

"As for the saved sect it is Ahlu Sunnah Wal Jamaah and there is no name for Ahlu Sunnah except one, and that is the people of hadith."

Al Ghunyatut Taalibeen p. 212

Ali ibn Al-Madini said:

"There are no people better than the companions of Hadith. The rest of the people were in search of the Dunya while they were establishing the Deen."

Masalat al Uloo wal Nazool p. 45

Ibn Abbas said:

"You will always see a man of Ahl as-Sunnah calling people to the Sunnah and forbidding bidah."

Al-Laalkaa'I in Sharh Usool I'tiqaad Ahl as-Sunnah

Bakr al Muzani said:

"If you want your prayer to be of benefit to you, say to yourself, "I might not have a chance to perform another prayer.""

Jaami Al-Uloom Wal-Hikam p. 466

Sufyaan Ath-Thawri said:

"If you hear that a man in the east is a follower of the Sunnah, then send salaams to him, for Ahl as-Sunnah are becoming very few."

Al-Laalkaa'I in Sharh Usool I'tiqaad Ahl as-Sunnah

Hatim bin Al Asim said:

"If a respectable good man sits with you, you would be watching every word you utter so that you do not say something wrong. Yet, you know that your words are watched by Allah but you still do not watch the words you utter!"

Aldaa Wa Al Dawaa, by Ibn al Qayyim

Imam Ahmad bin Hanbal said:

"whosoever reviles the Companions of the Prophet, then we do not believe he is safe from having rejected the Religion."

Imam Ahmad was asked concerning a Rafidi neighbor who greets him, should he answer his Salaam? He replied: "No"

Sunnah lil-Khilaal, 3/493

Abu Umamah Al Baheli said:

"On Judgment day, the slave of Allah will be given his book of deeds where he finds rewards for things he did not do, so he asks: O My Lord, where did I get these deeds? So Allah replies to him saying:"these are because of the people who backbited you and you did not know about it."

Aldaa Wa Al Dawaa by Ibn Al Qayyim

Abd al-Rahman bin Mahdi said:

"I dislike people to disobey Allah otherwise I would have wished everyone in this world to backbite me. There is no equal joy to find in your scale in the judgment day a deed you did not know about or even did."

Aldaa Wa Al Dawaa by Ibn Al Qayyim

Imam Malik said:

"The last generations of this ummah can only be reformed by that which reformed its first generations. What was not part of the religion then cannot become part of the religion now."

Ash Shifa by Al Qaadi Ayaad vol. 2 p.88

Salamah bin Dinar said:

"Hide your good deeds (from the people) just like you hide your evil deeds."

Abu Nu'aym, Bayhaqee

Malik ibn Dinar said:

"Whoever proposed to the world, then the world would not be satisfied until he gave up his Deen as dowry."

Al Bayhaqi, Al zuhd Al Kabeer p. 100

Once Umar ibn Abdul Azeez was advised:

"O Umar, beware of being the ally of Allah in open, while being his enemy in secret. If one's nature in open and secret do not equate then he is a hypocrite, and the hypocrites occupy the lowest level in Hellfire."

Al Bayhaqi, Al-Zuhd Al Kabeer p. 100

Ahmad ibn Harb said:

"There is nothing more beneficial to a Muslim's heart than to mix with the righteous and to watch their actions, while nothing is more harmful to the heart than mixing with the sinners and watching their actions."

Al Bayhaqi, Al Zuhd Al Kabeer p. 100

Muawiyah bin Murrah said:

"I lived during the time of seventy of the Companions of Muhammad and had they lived among you today, they would not recognize any of your acts except the Adhan!"

Hilyat Al Awliyaa 2/299

Abdul Kareem Al Jazari said:

"A pious man never debates."

Ash-Shuab, 8129

Qaasim al Joo'ee said:

"I advise you with five matters. When you are treated unjustly, do not behave unjustly; when you are praised do not become happy; when you are criticized do not become upset; when you are not believed do not become angry; and if the people act deceitfully towards you, do not act deceitfully towards them."

Related by Ibn al Jawzi in Sifatus as-Safwah 2/200

It is reported that a man was closely watching Bishr As-Sulaimi who was prolonging his prayer and praying it well. When Bishr completed his prayer, he said to the man:

"Do not be deceived by what you have seen from me. For indeed Iblis the Devil-may Allah curse him-worshipped Allah for thousands of years and then ended up being what he is now!"

Bahrud-Dumoo, p. 171

Umar ibn Al-Khattab once said to Al-Ahnaf ibn Qais:

"O Ahnaf, the more one laughs, the less dignity will he posses. Whoever jokes (excessively) is a person who will be taken lightly. Whoever does something frequently will become known by that thing. Whoever speaks often, errs often; the more often one errs, the less modesty will he possess; whoever has a low level of modesty will also have a low level of piety; and when one has a low level of piety, then his heart dies."

Sifatus-Safwah, 1/1449

It was said to imam Ahmad bin Hanbal:

"A man fasts, prays and stays inseclusion at the masjid, is that more beloved to you or if he speaks against the people of bida?"

He replied:

"If he fasts, prays and stays in seclusion he benefits only himself, but if he speaks against the people of innovation, that benefits all the muslims so that is better."

Majmoo Al-Fatawa

Abu Anas Hamad Al Uthman said:

"The evil of the Jews and Christians is open and clear to the common Muslims; as for the people of innovation, then their harm is not clear to every person...This is why the Scholars see that to refute the people of innovation takes precedence over refuting the Jews and Christians."

Zajarul Mutahawwin p. 96

Imam Ahmad said:

"Verily a person of theological rhetoric will never succeed, ever. You will never see anyone studying theological rhetoric, except that there is a corruption in his heart."

As-Sunnah p. 235

Imam Ahmad also said:

"Do not sit with the people of theological rhetoric, even if they defend the sunnah."

Manaaqibul Imaam Ahmad p. 205

Imam Al Awzaaee (d. 157) said:

"Adhere to the narrations from those who have preceded, even if the people reject you, and beware of the opinions of men, even if they beautify it with speech. So indeed the affair will become clear, while you are upon a straight path regarding it."

Bayhaqee in Al-Madkhal no.233

Abu Haatim Ar Raazee said:

"A sign of the people of innovation is their hatred of the people of narrations."

Ibnut Tabaree in As-Sunnah 1/189

Imam Ash Shaafie said:

"Stick to the people of hadith, since they are the most correct from amongst the people."

Siyar A'laamin Nubulaa, 10/60

Al Hasan Al Basri said:

"Do not sit with a person of innovation, for indeed he will put a disease in your heart."

Al-Itisaam of Ash Shaatibee, 1/172

Imam Zuhree said:

"The people of knowledge who came before us used to say 'Salvation lies in clinging to the sunnah'."

Ad-Daarimee, 96

Abu Darda said:

"Indeed my greatest fear concerning standing on the Day of Judgement is that it will be said to me: You have learned, hence what have you done with your knowledge?!"

Jaami'Bayaan al'Ilm wa Fadlih #647

Qaasim al Joo'ee said:

"Seize the benefit of five things from the people of your time: 1. When you are present, you are not known. 2.When you are absent, you are not missed. 3. When you are seen, your advice is not sought. 4. When you say something, your saying is not accepted. 5. When you have some knowledge, you are not given anything for it."

Related by Ibn al Jawzee in Sifatus Safwaa 2/200

Al Hasan al Basri said:

"If a man sits amongst people, and they perceive him to be ignorant, when in fact he is not ignorant, then this is truly the Muslim who possesses understanding (of the Religion)."

The Book of knowledge by Imaam Abu Khaithama An-Nisaa'ee #131

Abu Dharr al Ghafari said:

"Make in the world 2 gatherings, a gathering in search for the Hereafter, and a gathering in search for the halaal. The third type of gathering will harm you and not benefit you, so do not desire it."

Taken from al Hilyat al Awliya of Abu Nuaym

Abu Darda once said:

"Remember Allah in good times and He will mention you in hard times. When you remember those who have passed away, consider yourself like one of them. And when you think of involving yourself in some worldly matter, consider first what it will lead to in the end."

Al Dhahabi in Siyar A'lam Al Nubala

Abdullah ibn Masud said:

"A memoriser of the Quran should be known for his long night prayers when people are asleep, his fasting when people are eating, his sadness when people are happy, his silence when people are talking nonsense, and his humbleness when people are not. He should be wise, gentle and not talk too much, he should not be rude, negligent, clamorous nor hot tempered."

Ibn al Jawzee, Sifaat as Safwa 1/413

Ibn Kathir said:

"A characteristic of the dunya is that it flees from the one who chases her, and it chases the one who flees from her."

Tafsir Ibn Kathir 4/197

Al Khatib al Baghdaadee said:

"To the aalim, ignorance is seen as ignorance and to the Jaahil (grossly ignorant) knowledge is seen as ignorance."

Kitab al Faqih wa'l-Mutafaqqih 1/3

It was mentioned to Ahmad Ibn Hanbal that a man from the people of knowledge made a mistake and erred, and that he had repented from his mistake. So Imām Ahmad said:

"Allāh will not accept that from him until repentance and recantation from his [erroneous] saying is made apparent —and he announces that he said such-and-such, and that he has repented to Allāh, the most High, for his saying and has recanted from it. If he makes that apparent, then his repentance is accepted."

Then Ahmad Ibn Hanbal recited:

"Except for those who repent and make right their mistake and openly declare [the truth which they concealed]." (2:160)

Collected by Al-Hāfidh Ibn Rajab in Dhayl 'Alā Tabaqāt Al-Hanābilah, 1/300

Ibn Jawzi said:

"I believe that coming out of her house and roaming about the streets in itself is sufficient to cause trouble, let alone exhibiting her beauty and her body."

Ahkaam'un Nisa

Abdullah ibn Masood said:

"It is more beloved to me to bite onto a red coal until it cools, than for me to say about something that Allah has preordained, 'Only if it didn't happen'."

Az-Zuhd of Abu Dawood p. 136

Abu Masood al Balkhee said:

"Whoever is afflicted with tragedy and he rips up a garment or pounds on his chest then it is as if he has grabbed a spear and intends to fight his Lord, the Mighty and Majestic."

Faydul Qadeer, 3/230

Wahb ibn Munabbih said:

"whoever is afflicted with some type of calamity then Allah has put him through the path of the Prophets."

Al Hilyah 4/56

Al Awzaa'ee said:

"whoever stands the night in prayer, Allah will make easy for him his standing on the Day of Judgment."

Siyar A'laam an Nubalaa, 7/119

Ibrahim al Harbi said: 'I heard Ahmad ibn Hanbal say:

"If you love that Allah should keep you upon that which you love, then remain upon that which He loves, and the good is in the one who sees no good in himself."

Al-Aadaabush-Shariah 2/31 by Ibn Muflih

Umar ibn Abdul Azeez said:

"There is no excuse for anyone, after the Sunnah, to be misguided upon error which he thought was guidance."

As-Sunnah #95 of Al-Marwazee

Awzaa'ee said, in the explanation of the hadith of the strangers:

"Islam will not disappear, it is Ahlus Sunnah that will disappear to the point that there will only remain one of them in any one country."

Laalikaa'ee #19

Yunus ibn Ubayd said:

"It has come to the point that one who knows the Sunnah will think it something strange, and stranger than this person is who finds the Sunnah something familiar."

Laalikaa'ee #21 & Ibn Batta #20

Sufyan Ath-Thawri said:

"Treat Ahlus Sunnah well, for they are the strangers."

Laalikaa'ee #49

Ahmad ibn Harb stated:

"I worshipped Allah for 50 years, I wasn't able to find the sweetness of worship until I forsook 3 things: 1. I forsook seeking the acceptance of people, so I was able to speak the truth. 2. I forsook the companionship of the sinner, so I was able to accompany the righteous. 3. I forsook the sweetness of the life of this world, so I was able to find the sweetness of the afterlife."

Adh-Dhahabee, Siyar

Bishr ibn al Harith said:

"Look at the person who has the most piety, chastity and purest earning from the people and then accompany him and do not sit with the one who will not help you upon your life in the hereafter."

Ash-Shuab, 7/11197

Umar ibn al Khattab said:

"We used to say that this Ummah will be doomed by knowledgeable hypocrites."

Al Wilaayah Alaa Al Buldan 1/142

Abdul Wahhaab ibn Ziyaad said:

"I can't think of any deeds that are more virtuous than patience except for being pleased (with Allah and his predestination) and similarly I don't know of a level higher and nobler than being

pleased (with Allah and his predestination) and it is the head of loving Allah."

Al-Hilyah 6/163

Sufyan Ath Thawri said:

"3 qualities are from patience: not speaking about your misfortune, (not speaking about) your pain, and not praising yourself."

Al Hilyah 6/389

Umar ibn al Khattab would write to his governors:

"The most important of your affairs in my view is prayer; whoever prays regularly has protected his faith, but whoever neglects it, is bound to be more negligent in other issues of faith."

At-Taareeqah Al Hakamiyah p. 240

Umar ibn Abdul Azeez said:

"Allah never blesses a slave with a favour and then takes it away from him and then recompenses him in its place with patience, except that which He recompensed him with was better than what He took away from him."

Iddatus Saabireen p. 24

Yahyaa ibn Adam said:

"Paradise was surrounded by difficulties, and you dislike it, and Hellfire was surrounded by desires, and you run after it. You are like one who is afflicted with serious illness, if you are able to

patiently endure the pain of the cure, you will be healed, if not, the illness will only increase in severity."

"The Journey of the Strangers" by Al-Aajurree p. 67

Ibn Rajab said:

"All blessings are from Allah and His virtue, so whoever ascribes any of these blessings to other than Allah with the belief that it is not from Allah is a real Mushrik! And whoever ascribes these blessings to other than Allah with the belief that they are from Allah has committed hidden shirk."

Lataaif Al Maarif p.70

Concerning the strangers Ali said:

"They live in this world with their bodies but their souls are attached to heavenly matters, they are the ambassadors of Allah in His lands and His callers to His Religion. O how I desire to see them!"

Abu Nuaym 1/79

Umar ibn al Khattab said:

"Do not put off today's work until tomorrow, lest work accumulate and you achieve nothing."

Munaaqib Ameer Al Mumineen by ibn Jawzee p. 129

Al Hasan said:

"In this world the believer is like the stranger. He does not become upset when it degrades/humiliates him, nor does he

compete with others in chasing after its grandeur. For the people are in one state and his is in a totally different state."

Ahmad, Az-Zuhd p. 321

Sulaymaan would say when describing the strangers:

"Their intent is not the same as the rest of man, their desire for the Hereafter is not the same as the rest of man, and their supplications are not the same as the rest of man."

Abu Nuaym 9/256

Sulaymaan was asked about the greatest deed, he wept and said:

"That He(Allah) look at your heart and find it not desiring anything except Him of this world and the Hereafter."

Abu Nuaym 9/256

Umar ibn al khattab said:

"There is no relationship between Allah and anyone except through obedience to him."

Taareekh At-Tabaree, 4/306

Umar ibn al Khattab said:

"Ask Allah for help against your evil whims and desires just as you ask Him for help against your enemies."

Al-Faruq Umar ibn Al Khattab by Muhammad rasheed Rida, p. 119

Al Waki bin Al Jarrah reports:

We went out one Eid with Sufyaan ath Thawri and he said:

"The first thing we will do on this day of ours is to lower our gaze."

Ibn Abee al dunya, Kitaab Al-Wara article 66

Hassan ibn abee Sinaan went out one Eid and upon returning home his wife said:

"How many beautiful women have you looked at today?"

He said:

"Woe to you! I have looked at nothing but my toe from when I went out to when I returned to you."

Ibn Abee al Dunya, Kitaab Al-Wara article 68

Uthmaan ibn Hakeem said:

"Befriend the one who is above you in the religion and below you in the worldly life."

As-Samt, of Ibn Abee Dunya p. 45

Yahya ibn Katheer said:

"The best of brothers are those who say, 'Come let's fast before we die,' and the worst of brothers are those who say, 'Come let's eat and drink before we die.'"

Al-Hilyah 3/71

Hubayrah said:

"Consider the people based upon their friends."

Raudatul Uqalaa p. 108

Umar ibn al Khattab said:

"Whoever acts on whims and desires and sin loses out and harms no one but himself. Whoever follows the sunnah and adheres to laws and follows the right path, seeking that which is with Allah for those who obey Him, is doing the right thing and is a winner."

Taareekh At Tabaree 4/410

Abdullah ibn Masood said:

"Constantly look into the Mushaf."

Ash-Shuab p. 2028

Khaalid ibn Madaan said:

"When a door leading to good is opened up for one of you then he should hasten to it because you don't know when it will be shut."

Al Hilya 5/211

Bakr ibn Adullah Al Muzanee said:

"Whoever commits a sin laughing will enter the Fire crying."

Al Hilyah 6/185

Al Qaadhee Iyaad said:

"According to how small you look at the sin is how great it will be in the sight of Allah, and according to how greatly you look at the sin the smaller it will be in the sight of Allah."

As-Siyar 8/128

Abu Hazim Salamah ibn Dinar said:

"Look at every act that you would hate to die while committing, and then abandon it."

Al-Musannaf, 7/194

Ibn Abbas said:

"There cannot be a major sin along with seeking Allah's forgiveness, nor a minor sin while being persistant upon it."

Ash-Shu'ab 5/7268

Al Awzaa'ee said:

"It used to be said, 'From the major sins is for a man to do a sin and then look down upon it.'"

Ash-Shu'ab p. 6752

Abu Ayub al-Ansari said:

"Indeed a man will do a bad deed and be afraid of it so much that he will go to Allah in safety."

Ash-Shu'ab p.6880

Ibn al Mubarak said:

"Once Wuhayb ibn al Ward was asked 'Will the one who disobeys Allah find the sweetness of worship?' He replied: 'No, nor the one who even thinks about disobeying Allah.'"

Ash Shu'ab p. 833

Bishr ibn al Haarith said:

"You will not find the sweetness of worship until you place a barrier between yourself and your lusts."

As-Siyar, 10/473

Abul Hasan Al Muzayyan said:

"A sin committed after another sin is a punishment for the first sin and a good deed that is done after another good deed is the reward for the first good deed."

Sifatus Safwah 2/456

Umar bin al Khattab said:

"The one who is in a position of leadership is more likely to fall into temptation or sin, except those whom Allah protects, and they are few."

Futooh ash-Sham p. 100

Abdullah ibn Masood said:

"There isn't any true relaxation for the believers besides the meeting of Allah."

Az-Zuhd of Ahmed p. 194

Al Hasan al Basri said:

"Verily a man commits a sin and never forgets it and he won't cease to be afraid of it until he enters Paradise."

Az-Zuhd of Imam Ahmad p.338

Ahmad ibn Aasim said:

"Surely this is the easy prey, clean up the rest of your life and you will be forgiven for your past."

Az Zuhd al Kabeer p.228

Hasan said:

"The believer is the mirror of his brother, if he sees something that he is not pleased with, he straightens it out and adjusts it, and protects his honor in private and public."

Al-Ikhwaan of ibn Abid Dunya p. 55

Ibn al Qayyim said:

"The sinner does not care about whether he angers his Lord or not, all he cares about is satisfying his lusts and desires."

Ighaath Al-Lahafaan p.44

Ibn al Mubarak said:

"Whenever a man would see something from his brother that he dislikes, he would give him orders in private and forbid him in private. Conversely, he would be rewarded for him screening his brother and also rewarded for forbidding evil. As for today whenever a man sees what he dislikes he angers his brother and unveils his screen."

Raudatul Uqaalaa p. 197

Hasan al Basri said:

"The best attribute a believer can have is forgiveness."

Adab Shar'iyyah 11/121

Al Humaydee said:

"By Allah, that I should fight against those who reject the ahadeeth of Allah's Messenger is more beloved to me than that I should fight against a like number of Turks."

Siyar vol.10 p. 616-621

Bishr ibn Mansoor said:

"Verily, I think of something from the affairs of the worldly life which distracts me from thinking about the hereafter, and I fear upon my sanity."

Al-Hilyah 2/241

Abu ad-Dardaa said:

"You will not become an Aalim(scholar) until you become a muta'alim(student) and you will not become a muta'alim until you act upon the knowledge you posess."

Iqtidaa-u Al'Ilmi Al 'Amal, 29

Imam Malik was asked about the Raafidah and said:

"Do not speak to them (the Shia), nor relate from them, for indeed they lie."

Minhaaj As-Sunnah 1/13

Imam Ash Shafiee said:

"Among tht people who follow their own desires, I have not seen a group bear witness to more lies than the Rafidah."

Ikhtisaar Uloom al Hadith by Ibn Katheer p. 109

Qataadah ibn Khulayd said:

"You will never find a believer except doing one of three things:

1. Offering worship in the masjid.

2. Resting in a house that screens him.

3. Or handling some worldly business that is binding (on him)."

Sifatus Safwah 3/231

Abdullah ibn al Mutaz said:

"The knowledge of a hypocrite is in his speech, while the knowledge of a believer is in his actions."

Iqtidaa uAl'Ilmi Al'Amal, 38

Sufyaan Ath Thawri said:

"Knowledge knocks on the door of action: it enters if the door is opened, but leaves if it does not receive a reply."

Al-Muwafaqaat, 1/75

Abu Dardaa said:

"Woe to him who does not know, and seven times woe to him who knew but did not act!"

Ihyaa Uloom Ad-Deen 1/63

Abu Ubayd al-Qaasim ibn Salaam said:

"The follower of the Sunnah is like the one who holds onto hot coals. And today in my opinion, this is better than fighting with swords in the Cause of Allah."

Taateekh Baghdaad 12/410

Al Fudayl ibn Iyyad said:

"The souls are arrayed armies. So those that know one another will unite with one another, and those that don't know one another will be divided. And it is not possible for a person of the Sunnah to support a person of innovation except due to hypocrisy."

Sharrh Usool Itiqaad Ahlis Sunnah wal Jamaah 1/138

Yahya ibn Yahya an Naisaboori said:

"Defending the Sunnah is more virtuous than Jihad."

Naqd al Mantiq p.12

Hudhayfah ibn al Yamaan said:

"Every act of worship that the Companions of the Messenger did not do, do not do them."

Abu Dawood Sahih

Sufyaan ath Thawri said:

"Fear the trial and temptation of the ignorant worshipper and the evil corrupt scholar since their temptation is a trial for everyone that has been captivated and entraptured."

Al Jarh Wat Ta'deel, 1/91-92

Ibn Qudaamah said:

"The salaf used to forbid others from sitting with the innovators, looking into their books, and listening to their speech."

Al Adaab Ash Shariah 1/232

Ash Shawkaanee said:

"The Muslims have unanimously agreed that women are not allowed to go out of their homes with their faces uncovered, especially in places where there are many evil people."

Nayl Al-Awtaar, 6/226

Ibn al Jawzee said:

"A person who truly fears his Lord does not care about others and does not put himself in a position where his religion is at risk."

"Sincere counsel to students of Sacred Knowledge" by Ibn al Jawzee p. 72

Umar ibn al Khattab once wrote a letter to Abu Ubaydah ibn al Jarrah saying:

"It has reached me that the Muslim women enter the public wash areas along with the disbelieving women. So prevent this and do not allow it, for indeed it is not permissible for a disbelieving woman to see a Muslim woman uncovered."

Tafsir al Qurtubee 12/233

Imam Malik said:

"It is not allowed to take as a witness the innovators and people of desires."

Jaami Bayaan Al'Ilm wa Fadhlihi

Abu Shamah said:

"The order to stick to the Jamaah means sticking to the truth and its followers; even if those who stick to the truth are few and those who oppose it are many, since the truth is that which the first Jamaah from the time of the Prophet and his Comapnions were upon. No attention is given to the great number of the people of futility coming after them."

Al Baa'ith Alal-Bidah Wal Hawaadith p.19

Regarding the people of innovation, Imam Ahmad said:

"They differ concerning the Book, they are in opposition to the Book, and they all agree with each other in contradicting the Book. They use the unclear and ambiguous texts as proof for their views and they misguide the people because of what they have difficulty understanding."

Majmoo ar-Rasaail Al Kubra 1/106

Ibn al Qayyim said:

"Whoever obtains an authentic hadith from Allah's Messenger if he wants to turn away from it let him know that the Prophet is the one who is addressing you."

Madaarij Us-Salikeen

Ibn Abbas said:

"Allah has commanded the believing women, when they come out of their homes, due to a necessity, to cover their faces by placing their jalaabeeb over their heads, and only expose one eye."

Mukhtasar Tafsir Ibn Katheer 2/114

Muhammad ibn Sireen said:

"I asked Ubaydah As Salmani about Allah's saying "to cast jalaabeeb upon themselves" so he veiled his face and head and only exposed his left eye."

Tafsir Ibn Kathir 6/470

Umar ibn abdul Aziz said:

"Whoever acts without knowledge harms more than benefits."

Musannaf of Ibn Abi Shaybah 13/470

Ibn Hazm said:

"If you are impressed by your brothers' praise for you, then think of the criticism of your enemies, then your self-admiration will disperse. If you have no enemies, there is nothing good in you; there is no one whose status is lower than the one who has no enemy. It is no more than the status of the one wha has no blessing from Allah for which he is to be envied, may Allah keep us safe and sound. If you think little of your faults, then think of them if people found out about them. Imagine people finding out about them, then you will be embarrassed and will recognize your shortcomings."

Al Akhlaaq Was-Siyar p. 71

Ali ibn Abi Talib said:

"Serious matters are the best, and newly invented matters are the worst. Every newly invented matter is an innovation, and everyone who introduces something new is an innovator. The one who innovates is mislead, and no innovator introduces an innovation but he has forsaken a Sunnah."

Al Bidaayah Wan-Nihaayah, 7/319

Abaad ibn Abbad Al Khawwaas Ash-Shamee said:

"Let your attitude be, when finding something you disapprove of in your brothers, as though you are offering help from yourselves to yourselves."

Ad-Daarimee 1/160

Imam Abdur Rahman al Jauzi said:

"If you find a darkness in your heart after you sinned, know then that in your heart there is light, because of this light you felt the darkness."

Rowadathul Muhibeen 2/112

Ibn Hibban said:

"The best brothers are those who wish the most well for one. It is better to be hit by a person who wishes well for you than to be greeted by a bad one."

Ar-Rawdhah p.195

Ibn Hibban also said:

"The noble does not hurt the wise, he does not joke with the stupid and he does not mingle with the sinner."

Ar-Rawdah p.173

Sufyaan ath-Thawri said:

"Learn this knowledge and keep silent. Do not mix it with joking around lest the hearts spit it out."

As-Said p. 232

Ibn Rajab said:

"He who spreads his knowledge to the people and speaks to them must be very careful of not asking things from them. He must not be covetous for any of their wealth or provisions nor wish to win their hearts. He should just spread his knowledge and be content with not hoping anything from them through careful godliness. This is because greed of worldly matters and yearning for them are ugly traits especially when found in a scholar."

Quoted in his explanation of the hadith of Abu Darda, p.150-151

Umar ibn khattab said to Ziyad:

"Do you know what (things) destroy Islam? They are the death of a scholar, the Munafiq(hypocrite) who argues using the Quran, and the Imams who lead the people astray."

Ad-Daarimee 1/71

Hasan al Basri said:

"The Sunnah is - by Him besides whom none has the right to be worshipped – between those who exceed the limits and those who fall short. So be patient upon it, may Allah have mercy upon you. For indeed the Ahlus-Sunnah were a minority from those who preceded and shall be a minority from those to come. They did not accompany the people who are excessive when they exceeded the limits, nor the people of innovation when they innovated. Rather, they persevered upon the Sunnah, until they met their Lord."

Sunan ad-Darimi, Volume 1 pgs. 71-72

Abu Bakr said:

"Every step that a mujahid takes in the way of Allah earns him the merit of 700 good deeds and the forgiveness of 700 sins."

Tabari, 2/462

Abu Bakr also said:

"A people do not abandon Jihad in the way of Allah except that Allah abandons them, leaving them to be humiliated."

Al Bidaayah Wan-Nihaayah 6/305

Ibn al Qayyim said:

"The one who remains silent in the face of falsehood is a tongueless devil."

Ad Da'u wad-Dawaa

Sufyan Ath-Thawri said:

"Whoever loves that he should be asked, then he is not worthy of being asked."

Siyar A'laam Nubulaa 8/469

A man came to Aishah and asked: *"When will I know that I am pious?" She said: "When you realize that you are a sinner." He said: "And when will I realize I am a sinner?" She replied: "When you think you are pious."*

Tanbeeh Al-Ghafileen 251

Al Hasan al Basri said:

"The effect of learning in early age is like engraving on a stone."

Bahjat Al-Majaalis, 1/109

Al Awzaa'ee said:*"It used to be said that there were five things that the companions of Muhammad and those who followed them in goodness were upon:*

1. Sticking to the Jamaah.

2. Following the Sunnah.

3. Maintaining the masjids.

4. Reciting the Quran

5. Making Jihad in Allah's cause."

Hilyah, 8/142

Sa'eed ibn Jubayr said:

"For my son to accompany a wicked sinner is more beloved to me than for him to accompany an innovator who performs great worship."

Ash-Sharh Wal-Ibaanah, p. 149

Matr Al-Warraq said:

"A few deeds from the sunnah is better than many deeds of bidah. Whoever performs a deed from the sunnah, Allah will aaccept it from him. And whoever performs an act of bidah, Allah will reject his bidah."

Hilyah 3/76

Al Hasan al Basri said:

"The believer combines perfection (in worship) and fear (that his deeds will be rejected); and the hypocrite combines between evil (deeds) and feeling safe from (Allah's punishment)."

Madaarij As-Saalikeen 1/512

Yahya ibn abi Kathir said:

"Learn the intention, for it is more serious than the action."

Jaamiul Uloom wal Hikam p. 34

Hishaam bin Urwa used to say:

"Do not question the people about what they have innovated today because they have prepared answers for it, rather ask them about the sunnah because they do not know it."

Imam Aloosi in Ghayatul Amaanee Fi Radd Alan-Nabahaanee 1/367

Ibn 'Ijlan said:

"Allah made the believer's strength in his heart and did not make it in his limbs, don't you see a weak old man fast the hot days and stand (in prayer) at night while a young man is unable to do that."

Sifat Al Safwa 3/341

Faatimah, daughter of the Prophet, said:

"The best women are those who do not see the men, and who are not seen by the men."

Ahkaam An-Nisaa, p.219

Ali ibn abi Talib said:

"Whoever read the Quran and dies and enters hell, is among those who used to take the verses of Allah in jest."

Al Mustatraf 1/29

Ali ibn abi Talib also said:

"I would not forsake the Sunnah of the Prophet for the opinion of anyone."

Fath Al Baari 2/421

Hasan al Basri said:

"I met some people who would not rejoice at tht splendor of life when it came to them, nor dedicate their attention to any part of it that went away from them. This life was as worthless in ther eyes as dust. One of them lived for fifty or sixty years during which he only owned the clothes that he wore, did not have a barrier between his body and the floor when he slept, and did not ask his family to cook a dish of food for him. When night came, they would be standing and then laying their foreheads on the floor (in Sujud[prostration]), with tears running down their cheeks. They begged their Lord to free their necks (from the Fire). Whenever they performed a good deed, they appreciated Allah for it and asked Him in supplication to accept it. Whenever they commited an error they felt sad and begged Allah to forgive it for them, may Allah's mercy and pleasure be on them. By Allah! They were not saved from the repercussions and evil consequences of sins, except through Allah's forgiveness."

Al Ihya, vol. 4 p.239

Al Bayhaqi said:

"As for wiping the face with the hands after concluding the supplication, I do not know that any of the Salaf did it."

As-Sunan 1/212

Imam Ash Shafie said:

"Muslims have a consensus that when a sunnah from Allah's Messenger becomes clear to a person, it is not permissible for him to leave it for anybody's opinion."

Ar-Risaalah

Abu Ubayd al Asqalaani said:

"I have not seen Abu Ubaydah Al-Khawas laugh for forty years. It was said to him: "Why don't you laugh?" He said: "How can I laugh while a Muslim is still imprisoned by the Mushrikeen?"

Sifat Al Safwah 2/416

Sufyan bin Uyaynah said:

"When your private (conduct) is the same as your public, then that is good character, when your privacy is better than your public appearance then that is virtue, and when your public appearance is better than you private, then transgression."

Tarikh Baghdad 13/173

Al Fudayl bin Iyad said:

"Forsaking action for the sake of other people is to seek their admiration. To act for the sake of their admiration is to associate others with Allah. Devotion is when Allah frees you from both of these states."

p. 6-7, Ibn Rajab, Ibn al-Qayyim, al-Ghazali, The Purification of the Soul. Al-Firdous Ltd. London:1993.

Ayyub said:
"It is much harder for the people of action to purify their intentions than it is to execute any of their actions."

p. 6, Ibn Rajab, Ibn al-Qayyim, al-Ghazali, The Purification of the Soul. Al-Firdous Ltd. London:1993.

Ibn al Qayyim said:

"The best deed to achieve the pleasure of your Lord in every moment is that which is required and dictated by that time."

Madarij al-Salikin

Maruf al Karkhi said:
"Hoping to receive the Mercy of the One who you insist on being disobedient to is a kind of betrayal and foolishness."

Hilyah al-Awliya' (8/367)

Ibn al Qayyim said:

"A sincere advisor does not have enmity towards you if you do not accept his advice."

Ar-Rooh, Page 233

Al Awza'i said:

"The major sins are the sins one commits, then considers them insignificant and underrates them."

p. 51, Talib Ibn Tyson al-Birtani, Purify My Heart. Dar-us-Salam Publications. Riyadh:2012

al Hasan al Basri said:

"The land of Paradise is flat and angels keep planting on it. When they slacken, they are asked "Why did you slacken?" They [the

angels] say, 'Our fellow has slackened.' Do not make angels feel slackened, may Allah bestow His Mercy on all of you."

Hilyatu'l-Auliyaa by Abu-Nu'aym (9/276), who attributed this narration to Abu Sulayman ad-Darani

Al Junaid al Baghdadi said:

"If a man worships Allah for one thousand years, and then he turns away from him for one moment, then what he missed in this moment is more than what he gained [in the one thousand years of worship]."

Hilyatu'l-Auliyaa by Abu-Nu'aym (10/278)

Sa'eed bin al Musayyab said:

"The servants never honor themselves with anything better than acts of obedience to Allah, and they never humiliate themselves with anything worse than disobeying Allah. It is enough victory for a believer to see his enemy disobeying Allah."

Sifah As-Safwah 2/81

As-Sariy said:

"Make your grave your treasury, which you fill with as much good works as you can. When you end up in it, you will surely be pleased with what it has kept for you."

Az-Zuhd, by al-Baihaqi, p. 229

Ibn Taymiyyah said:

"If one attains (what he desires), he is pleased and if he is unable to attain it, he becomes discontented. Such a person is a slave ['abd] to the things he desires. He is a slave of it, since true slavery and servitude are the enslavement and servitude of the heart."

Ibn Taymiyyah's Essay on Worship, p. 100-101

Sa'eed bin Jubayr said:

"Dhikr is obedience to Allah. Whoever obeys Allah has in fact remembered Him. Whoever does not obey Him is not one who remembers Him, even if he says tasbeeh, and recites the Qur'an a lot."

Sharh as-Sunnah, al-Baghawee, vol. 5, p.10

Imam Ahmad bin Hanbal said:

"For everything there is a blessing; the blessing of the hearts is being pleased with Allah, the Almighty, the All-Powerful."

Manaqib Al-Imam Ahmad by ibn al-Jawzi, p. 276

Sufyan ath Thawri said:

"And beware of showing hypocritical piety — piety that you do not really feel, and beware of showing piety on your face when you do not feel it in your heart."

Hilyatul-Auliyaa, by Abu Na'eem al-Asbahaanee (7/48)

Ibn al Jawzi said:

"Know that the heart of a person of sound mind cannot be free of sadness, because he remembers his previous sins, therefore becomes sad, he thinks about his negligence, reflects on what the scholars and the righteous have said, as a result he becomes sad for not taking heed."

p. 69, Ibn al-Jawzi, Disciplining The Soul. Daar as-Sunnah Publishers. Birmingham: 2011.

Hasan al Basri said:

"Know that you cannot love Allah until you love obeying Him!"

Pg. 49 of "The Key to Paradise" by Ibn Rajab al Hanbali Daar us-Sunnah publishers 2007

Abu Hazim Salamah bin Dinar said:

"No servant of Allah mends what is between him and Allah, except that Allah mends what is between him and other servants. And he does not spoil what is between him and Allah, except that Allah spoils what is between him and the servants of Allah. Working for the sake of ones face is easier than working for the sake of all faces. For if you work for the sake of that Face [the Face of Allah], all faces will turn to you. But if you spoil it, all faces will the detest you."

Abu Nu'aym, al-Hilya (3:239)

Ibn al Qayyim said:

"The inner reality of veneration for a Divine Law is to follow it with neither excessive license nor excessive strictness. The goal is the straight path that leads the one who travels it to God. But there is not one of God's commandments without two ways of approach to the devil: one by deficiency, the other by excess. And it makes no difference which of the two errors overtakes the servant: they appear in his heart as equals."

p. 15, Ibn Qayyim al-Jawziyya, The Invocation of God. The Islamic Texts Society. UK:2000.

Hudhayfah bin Qatadah al Mar'ashiyy said:

"If you don't fear for the possibility of God's punishment for the greatest of your deeds, then you are destroyed."

Imām al-Dhahabī, Siyar Aʿlām al-Nubalāʾ

Hudhayfah bin Qatadah al Mar'ashiyy also said:

"If only I had found somebody who truly hates me for the sake of Allah, I would have made it mandatory upon myself to love him."

Imām al-Dhahabī, Siyar Aʿlām al-Nubalāʾ 9/283

Sufyan bin Uyaynah said:

"What the slave detests is better for him than what he loves! This is because what he detests will cause him to increase in his dua,

whereas what he loves will distract him (from worshiping Allah)."

Al-Hamad, p. 101

Al Ala bin Ziyad said:

"One of you should consider that death has come to him, that he asked Allah for respite and He gave him respite. So, let him use this time working in Allah's obedience."

Sifatu as-Safwah, vol. 3, p. 224

Sa'eed bin Masud said:

"Abandoning excesses in life is hard, but abandoning Paradise is harder. Know that the mahr (bridal-money) for Paradise requires abandoning this life."

Tanbihul-Ghafilin, vol. 1, p. 85

Sa'eed bin Masud also said:

"If you see the slave feel content when his wealth increases and his Hereafter decreases, then know that he is the cheated one who is being toyed with in his own face, but is unaware of what's happening to him."

Mukashafatul-Qulub, p. 157

Muhammad bin Wasi' said:

"If you see a man crying in Paradise, would you not be surprised at his crying?" He was answered in the affirmative. So he asked them again, "What is more surprising is he who laughs in this life, while utterly unaware where his final destination will be!"

Al-Ihya, vol. 3, p. 137

Muhammad bin Sauqah said:

"If we were only tested with these two characteristics, we would deserve the punishment: one of us becomes richer and he delights, even though Allah did not witness from him a delight like it before with regards to a religious blessing he earned. One of us suffers a loss and grieves more so than whatever Allah witnessed from him of grief for a loss he suffered in his religion."

Hilyatul-Auliya', vol. 5, p. 4

Salman bin Dinar said:

"Whatever you would like to accompany you in the Hereafter, plant it today, and whatever you hate to accompany you in the Hereafter, then abandon it today."

Sifatus-Safwah, vol. 2, p. 166

Abu Hazim Salamah bin Dinar said:

"If the way to enter Paradise is by abandoning all what one loves in this life, Paradise will still be worth the price. What about it if one might enter Paradise by leaving one part out of a thousand

parts of what one loves in life? What about it if one might be saved from the Fire by enduring one part of a thousand parts of what he hates to endure life?"

Tanbihul-Ghafilin, vol. 1, p. 85

Umar ibn al Khattab said:

"Woe to he to whom this life represents his hope and sins are his deeds, whose appetite is tremendous, whose wisdom is minute, who has knowledge in this life but is ignorant in the Hereafter."

Al-'Aqibah, p. 90

Al Hasan al Basri said:

"Amazing is he who laughs, even though the fire is in front of him, and he feels elation, while death is awaiting him!"

Tanbihul-Ghafilin, vol. 1, p. 212

Umar bin abdul Aziz said:

"You were created to remain forever, but will be transferred from one life to another. Oh Allah's slaves, you now live in a life that contains food, but often brings pain in the throat while swallowing it, and contains drinks, but you often choke while drinking. This life is does not bring you a delight that comforts you, but takes away another delight, that you hate to lose. Therefore, work for the life to come where you will end up for eternity."

Al-Ihya', vol. 3, p.288

Dirar bin Murrah said:

"Iblis (satan) said, "If I win three things from the son of Adam, I will have earned what I wanted from him: if he forgets his sins, thinks high of his actions, and becomes fond of his opinion.""

Sifatus-Safwah vol. 3, p. 116

Auf bin Abdullah said:

"Those who were before you would leave for this life what remained with them after taking care of their Hereafter. You, on the other hand, leave for your Hereafter what remains after taking care of your life."

Sifatus-Safwah, vol. 3, p. 101

Al Fudayl bin Iyad said:

"The slave's fear of Allah is as substantial as his knowledge of Him, and his disinterest in this life is as substantial as his interest in the Hereafter."

As-Siyar, vol. 8, p.426

Ibn al Qayyim said:

"And to have spent the night sleeping and awoken regretful is better than to have spent the night standing (in prayer) and awaken impressed with oneself."

Madarij as-Saalikeen, Volume 1, p.183

Al Hasan al Basri said:

"A person may struggle in the way of God, without ever striking a sword even once."

Tafsīr Ibn Kathīr, commentary on al-Ankabut:6

Umar ibn al Khattab said:

"If a man comes out of his house carrying a burden of sins like the mountains of Tihamah, then when he hears some knowledge he fears Allah and repents, he will go back home with no sins on him. So do not forsake the gatherings of the scholars."

Miftah Dar as-Sa'adah, 1/122; Fara'id al-Kalam, p. 135.

Hasan al Basri said:

"Whoever realizes that death is his ultimate fate, Judgement his final appointment, and standing before Allah his inevitable witnessing, then it is his right that in this world, his grief be prolonged."

Fath al-Bari

Al-Hasan Al-Basri wrote to Caliph 'Umar bin Abdul-Aziz:

"This life is temporary and not permanent; Adam was sent down to it as punishment. Therefore, O Leader of the Faithful, beware of this life and know that the best provision pertains to abandoning excessive indulgence in it and that wealth pertains to being deprived of its splendor. This life always has its victims. It brings disgrace to those who are mighty in it and poverty to those who collect it with greed. Its parable is poisons: when one unknowingly eats the poison, he will die as a consequence. Therefore, be like a wounded man who nurses his wounds for a while for fear of extended repercussions and endures the bitterness of the medicine so that his illness is not prolonged. Beware of this deceiving life, for it cheats and lures people with its beauty. Life lures with its false adornments and deceives with its hopes. It has beautified itself for those who seek it in marriage and became just like the beautiful bride at whom the eyes stare, whom the hearts adore and the inner self covets. However, life kills all of its husbands. Yet, its current husbands do not take a lesson from the fate of her ex-husbands whom it killed, nor do the latter advise the surviving former against its danger. Whoever covets life, satisfies his desire from it and becomes further deceived by his excessive indulgence in its affairs. He becomes a tyrant who forgets the Return (to Allah), until his feet are removed from this life, and consequently, his sorrow increases and his grief intensifies. He departs this life without sufficient provisions and is introduced to the Last Life without having firm foundation to rely on. Beware of this life, O Leader of the Faithful! Even when you feel more delight in it as ever before, you should be more aware of it as ever before. Whenever owners of life's splendor feel comfortable in this life, it is followed with an affliction. What seems delightful in this life is connected to hardship, and whatever is thought permanent, is bound to

vanish. The joys of this Life are mixed with sadness. Whatever leaves it never comes back and whatever is to come is unknown, so awaiting for it does not avail. Its wishes are unreal, its hopes are false, its core is impure and its essence is encompassed by grief. Verily, the son of Adam is always in danger from this life while still in it. Life was offered to your Prophet Muhammad with its keys and treasures, but he refused to accept it. He disliked to covet what Allah does not prefer, or to elevate what His King has made lowly. It is Allah Who kept life's splendor away from the righteous as a test for them and gave its abundance to His enemies as a trial from Him. It was reported that Allah the Exalted and Most Honored said to Moses 'If you see riches coming, say, 'this is on account of a sin for which the punishment is sent sooner rather than later.' If you see poverty coming, say, 'Welcome, O sign of the righteous."

Iddatus-Sabirin, p.331

Umar bin Khattab said:

"Do not speak about that which does not concern you. Know your enemy and be wary of your friend, except for the trustworthy one. And no one is trustworthy, except for the person who fears Allah. Do not walk with the evildoer, lest he teaches you some of his wickedness; and do not reveal your secrets to him. And when you consult others in your affairs, consult only those who fear Allah."

Sifatus-Safwah 1/149

Imam ash-Shafi'ee said the following verses describing this world and its people:

"It is no more than a carcass, for which dogs compete to snatch away. If you avoid it, they will not harm you, and if you snatch a piece away, they will struggle with you."

Kashf al-Khufaa' of ash-Shaykh Isma'eel ibn Muhammad al-'Ajalooni (1/40) and (1/410)

Imam Ibn Taymiyyah said:

"Rather, wealth should be viewed just like the toilet, in that you have need for it and resort to it when necessary, but it has no place in your heart."

Majmoo' al-Fatawa (10/663)

Hasan al Basri said:

"*O people, prepare for departure, for very little time remains from this world. Prepare to move, for there is no way to stay here. Do you not know that you will soon be surrendered to the place of trial? Do you not know that each one of you will soon be alone with his deeds and that you will be presented to Allah on the Day of Judgment? He ordered you obey Him, but you have not obeyed Him. He forbade you from sinning, but you have not desisted from perpetrating. He has (threatened) you with the Hell-fire, but you are neither afraid nor terrified of it. He has encouraged you to seek out Paradise, but you do not desire it or long for it. Your white hairs are warning you of approaching death, so what are you waitin for? O white haired one, you are able to perform good deeds, so what is your excuse. O one who obeys his mouth and his desires, who wastes his share of the Hereafter by taking his entire share in this world, who persists in perpetrating sins and evil deeds-would that I knew: what will your excuse be when you stand before Him? What argument will you put forth when you go to Him? You are lost and misguided, so ask Allah, the All-Mighty , to forgive me and you."*

Al Mawaiz wal Majalis page 181

Imam Ibn ul-Qayyim said:

"When there is money in your hand and not in your heart, it will not harm you even if it is a lot; and when it is in your heart, it will harm you even if there is none in your hands."

Madaarij al-Saalikeen, 1/463

Ibn ul-Jawzi said:

"The most virtuous of affairs is to increase in knowledge, for indeed the one who limits himself to what he knows and considers it sufficient will become opinionated; and exalting himself will become an obstacle for him in benefiting and his error will become clarified for him through revision. And it may be that he was exalted within himself and was not bold enough to repel it."

Saydul-Khaatir (81)

Abu ad-Dardaa said:

"Everyone falls short of his wisdom and knowledge sometimes. If this life brought him an increase in money, he becomes happy and elated. Meanwhile, the nights and the days keep decreasing his life term, but he does not become sad on account of this decrease. What good will the increases in wealth bring, when the life-term is ever decreasing?"

Siyar A'laam an-Nubalaa (19/483)

Sufyaan Ibn 'Uyaynah said:

"Whoever seeks knowledge then he has pledged allegiance to Allaah."

Madaarij al-Saalikeen, 2/470

Imam Ibn ul-Qayyim said:

"If your aim is piety, other aims are never missed."

al-Fawaaid

Imam Ibn Taymiyyah said:

"The sign of the people of bid'ah is that they do not follow the salaf."

Majmoo' al-Fatawa (4/155)

Imam Ibn ul-Qayyim said:

"Sins are wounds and one wound may cause death."

al-Fawaaid

Imam Ahmad ibn Hambal said:

"It was said to Imaam Ahmad: 'May Allaah reward you for the good you have (done) for Islaam.' He said: 'Rather, Allaah has (done) good for me through Islaam. Who am I, and what am I?'"

Siyar A'laam an-Nubalaa (11/225)

Imam Ibn ul-Qayyim said:

"The most precious reward during life is to busy yourself with most suitable and useful matters in their exact and suitable time. How can he be rational who sells Paradise and what is in it, for one hour of passing pleasure?"

al-Fawaaid

Sufyan Ath-Thawri said:

"Verily, when Allah withholds, He actually gives, because He did not withhold on account of miserliness or stinginess, but rather He looked at the benefit of the servant. So the fact that He withheld is actually His choice for the servant and His excellent decision."

Madaarij al-Saalikeen, 2/215

Muhammad ibn Abdul Wahhaab said:

"What is the worth of the religion to you? What is Allah's pleasure and Paradise worth to you? What is Allah's Hell and wrath worth to you? Flee with your religion, for Paradise and Hell are in front of you."

Abdul-Mushin ibn Baaz in Rasaail al-Imaam Muhammad ibn Abdil-Wahhaab al-Shakhsiyyah: Diraasah Daawiyyah, vol. 1, pp. 126-127

Imam Ibn ul-Qayyim said:

"Optional knowledge is better than the excellence of extra and optional worship. This is because the benefit of knowledge is general, it benefits its possessor and it benefits the rest of the people as well. Whereas the benefit of worship is particular to the person who does that worship. Also because with the scholar, his benefit and knowledge remains after his death. Whereas worship is cut off from him at his death."

Miftaah daaris Sa'aadah, 1/120

Imam Ibn ul-Qayyim said:

"If bid'ah only consisted of Lies, then it would not have been accepted and everybody would even hurry to condemn it and refute it. And if it only consisted of Haqq (truth), then it would not have been a Bid'ah, rather, in agreement with the Sunnah, but it (Bid'ah) consist of both truth and lies in which the truth is clothed with lies."

as-Sawaa'iq al-Mursalah (3/925)

Imam Ibn Taymiyyah said:

"Sins are like chains and locks preventing their perpetrator from roaming the vast garden of tawhid and reaping the fruits of righteous actions."

Majmoo' al-Fatawa (14/49)

Imam Ibn ul-Qayyim said:

"O you who spends his lifetime in disobeying his Lord! No one amongst your enemies is wicked to you than you are to yourself."

al-Fawaaid

Imam Ibn ul-Qayyim said:

"By Allaah! The enemy did not wrong you except after the Lord abandoned you, so do not think that Shaytaan overpowers you, it is just the Maintainer (i.e. Allaah) who has forsaken you."

al-Fawaaid

Imam Adh Dhahabee said:

"That which a scholar needs to be is:

-Taqiyan (have taqwah)

-Thakiyah (have intelligence)

-Nahwiyan (firm in Arabic grammar)

-Lugawiyan (firm in Arabic language)

-Zakiyan (pure in action and/or intentions)

-Hayiyan (shy)

-Salafiyan (follow the way of the Salaf As Saleh)...."

Siyar A'laam an-Nubalaa (13/380)

Ibn ‘Aqeel al-Hanbali said:

“It is not permissible for me to waste an hour of my life even when my tongue is not busy with memorizing or debating with others, or my eyes are not busy in reading. I would think even when I am resting or relaxing, so I would not get up without an idea to write down. I limit the time I spend eating as much as I can, to such an extent that I choose a few crumbs and follow it with water rather than bread, because bread takes more time to chew, so as to save my time for reading or writing down some useful ideas. The best thing for the wise man to save, is time.”

Salaah al-Ummah (4/169-175)

Imam al-Barbahaaree said:

“Beware of small innovations, because they grow and become large. This was the case with every innovation introduced into this Ummah. It started as something small, bearing a resemblance to the truth, which is why those who entered into it were misled, and then were unable to leave it. So it grew and it became the religion which they followed, so they deviated from the Straight Path and thus left Islaam. May Allaah have mercy upon you! Examine carefully the speech of everyone you hear from, in your time particularly. So do not act in haste, nor enter into anything from it, until you ask and see: Did any of the Companions of the Prophet sallallaahu ‘alayhi wa sallam speak about it, or any of the (early) Scholars? So if you find a narration from them about it, cling to it and do not go beyond it for anything, nor give precedence to anything over it and thus fall into the Fire.”

Sharh us-Sunnah (no. 8) of Imam al-Barbahaaree

Abdulrahman al-Kawakibi said:

The commoners are the strength of the oppressor and his force. Through them and upon them he runs rampant. He imprisons them, so they cheer for his might; He takes their wealth unjustly, so they praise him for having spared their lives; He insults them, so they admire his high rank; He tempts some of them against others, so they find pride in his policies; When he spends their money wastefully, they say: How Generous!; And if he kills from them but does not maim, they consider him Merciful; He drags them to the dangers of death, and they obey him out of fear that they would be reprimanded; If a few of those with dignity resented him, he fights them as if they were transgressors. What results is that these commoners slaughter themselves with their own hands because of this fear which develops from their ignorance and foolishness. If that ignorance was to alleviate, and the mind was to become enlightened, then that fear would go away and the people would habitually no longer follow except that which would bring them benefit, as the saying goes: A wise person only serves himself. At that time, the oppressor would have to either retire or straighten [himself].

Tabai' al-Istibdad wa-Masari' al-Isti'bad (p. 37)

Sufyan al-Thawri said one day to his companions:

"*Tell me, If among you was someone who transmitted whatever you said to the Sultan, would you have spoken out about anything?*"

They said: No

So he said:

Then [know that] indeed with you are those who transmit your speech to Allah -Glorified and Exalted is He-!

{Not a word does he (or she) utter, but there is a watcher by him ready (to record it).} [Qaaf 50:18]

Al-Tabsera by ibn jawzi 2/237

Imam Ibn Taymiyyah said:

"The Imaams of the Sunnah and the Jamaa'ah, and the people of knowledge and eemaan (faith) have in them 'adl (justice), 'ilm (knowledge) and rahmah (mercy), and they know the truth which conforms to the Sunnah and which is free from innovations. They do justice to those who depart from the Sunnah and the Jamaa'ah, even if they have been wronged, just as Allaah – the Most High – said: "O you who believe!! Stand out firmly for Allaah and be witnesses, and do not let the hatred of others swerve you away from doing justice. But be just! That is closer to taqwaa (piety)." [Soorah al-Maa'idah 5:8]. Likewise, they are merciful to the creation; desiring for them goodness guidance and knowledge. They never intend for them any harm or evil. Rather, when they criticise them and explain to them their error, ignorance or wrong-doing, then their purpose in doing so is only to clarify the truth, and to be merciful to the creation, to enjoin the good and forbid the evil, and to make the word of Allaah uppermost so that the way of life becomes purely for Allaah."

Radd 'alal-Bakree (p.256)

Yahya ibn Hubayra said:

Time is the most precious thing you should safeguard.

And yet I see it the easiest thing you lose.

Zayl Tabaqaat Al-Hanabila (1/182)

Alaa Ibn Musayyib said:

"Khaytham used to place bags of money in the masjid and sit, so if he saw one of his friends wearing raggedy clothing, he would give him a bag of money."

Al-Ikhwaan, p.224

Farwah Ibn naufal said:

"Once I was with Khabbaab (ra), so we went out to the masjid and he grabbed my hand and said to me, 'Seek nearness unto Allaah to the best of your ability for surely you cannot get close to Him with something more beloved to Him than His Speech.' "

Ash-Shu'ab, p.1463

Khaalid Ibn Ma'daan said:

"When a door leading to good is opened up for one of you then he should hasten to it because you don't know when it will be shut."

Al-Hilya, 5/211

Bakr Ibn 'Abdillaah Al-Muzanee said:

"Whoever commits a sin laughing will enter the Fire crying."

Al-Hilyah, 6/185

Abu Haatim said:

"Probing and seeking the faults of others is from the branches of hypocrisy just like thinking good of others is from the branches of faith. The intelligent one always has a good opinion of his brothers, and keeps his grief and sadness to himself. As for the ignorant one, he has evil opinion of his brothers and does not think about his crimes and distress."

Siyar A'lam an-Nubalaa

Umar Ibn Al-Khattaab said:

"Whoever appoints a man because of favouritism or blood ties, and does not appoint him for any other reason, has betrayed Allaah and His Messenger. And whoever appoints an evildoer knowing that he is an evildoer, is just like him."

Al-Idaarah Al-'Askariyah Fee Ad-Dawlat Al-Islaamiyah, 1/66

Al Shatibi said:

"One of the last things to leave the hearts of the righteous is the: Love of leadership and authority."

Al-I'tisaam – al-Shatibi

Umar Ibn Al-Khattaab said:

"Do not think badly of a word uttered by your brother, when you can find a good interpretation for it."

Majmoo' Fataawa Ibn Baaz, 26/365

Ahmad Ibn Harb said:

"Verily one of us prefers shade over standing in the sun, but we won't prefer Paradise over the Fire!"

Al-Ihyaa, 4/568

Abdullaah Ibn Mas'ood said:

"There isn't any true relaxation for the believers besides the meeting of Allaah."

Az-Zuhd of Ahmad, p.194

Imaam Ash-Shaafi'ee said:

"It is 'deemed as forbidden' to plaster graves and to write on them the name of the person within the grave and the likes. It is also 'deemed as forbidden' to build on them."

Al-Majmoo' 5/266

Imaam Ash-Shaafi'ee also said:

"I have seen from the leaders those of them who destroy whatever has been built on graves and the fuqahaa did not see any problem in what the leaders did."

Al-Muhadhdhab, 1/456

Abdul Wahhaab Ibn Ziyaad said:

"I can't think of any deeds that are more virtuous than patience except for being pleased [with Allaah and Qadar] and similarly I don't know of a level higher and nobler than being pleased [with Allaah and Qadar] and it is the head of loving Allaah."

Al-Hilyah, 6/163

Umar Ibn 'Abdul-'Azeez said:

"Allaah never blesses a slave with a favour and then takes it away form him and then recompenses him in its place with patience, except that which He recompensed him with [patience] was better than what He took away from him."

Iddatus Saabireen, p. 24

Yahyaa Ibn Mu'aadh Al-Raazee said:

"Son of Aadam; you seek the world as if your very life depended on it and you seek the Hereafter as if you have no need of it! You will acquire what you need from this world even if you do not run after it, but you will only attain the Hereafter if you run after it. So be aware of your true condition!"

"The Journey Of The Strangers", By Al-Aajurree, p. 67

Yoonus Ibn 'Ubayd said:

"How amazing is the one who calls to the sunnah today! And what is even more amazing than him is the one who answers the call to the Sunnah!"

Sharh us-Sunnah (no. 127) of Imam al-Barbahaaree

Ibn al-Mubaarak said:

"How many deeds few in number have become many by way of the niyyah (intention) and how many deeds great in number have been made insignificant due to a (faulty) intention."

Siyar A'laam an-Nubalaa (8/400)

Al-Imaam Al Awzaa'ee said:

"We used to joke and laugh but when people began to immitate us, I feared to even smile."

Siyar A'laam an-Nubalaa (7/132)

Hamdoon Al-Qassaar was asked:

"Why is the speech of the Salaf more beneficial than ours?' He replied: 'This is because they spoke to give ascendancy to Islam and to please The Most Merciful; whereas we speak to give ascendancy to ourselves, to seek after the worldly life and please the creation."

Safwatus Safwah: 2/122

Abu Al-Qasim Al-Junaid said:

"The reality of Truthfulness [and Honestly] is to be truthful in instances when nothing can save you except lying."

Mawaa'iz al-Imam al-Junaid p. 29

Abu 'Uthman Al-Jeezi said:

"From the signs of Happiness is that you obey Allah and you are afraid that it will not be accepted, and from the signs of Misery is that you disobey Allah and hope that you will be saved."

Fath Al-Bari 11/301

Abu Amr al-Awzaa'i said:

"If innovations appear, and the People of Knowledge do not denounce [and reject] it, it will soon become a Sunnah!"

Sharaf Ashaab Al-Hadeeth by al-Khateeb al-Baghdadi, p. 17

Hasan al Basri said:

"When a fitnah first approaches, every scholar recognizes it, and only when it dies away does every ignorant come to know of it."

"The way out of Tribulations" by Muhammad Ismail al Muqaddam pg. 11

Abu 'Amr Al-Awzaa'i said:

"Keep yourself patient upon the Sunnah, and stop where those before you have stopped ... Say what they have said, and refrain from what they have refrained from.

Follow the path of your righteous Salaf, since what sufficed them would surely suffice you.

Imaan (Faith/Belief) would never be upright without Words ...

And Words would never be upright without Action/Deeds ...

And neither the Words nor the Actions would ever be upright without an intention that is in accordance with the Sunnah.

Those who have passed from among our Salaf did not distinguish between Imaan and Action, for Action is from Imaan, just as Imaan is from Action.

Imaan is but a comprehensive name, just as the [specifics of these] Religions are gathered under their names, and is proven through action.

So whoever believed with his tongue, and knew with his Heart, and validated that with his Actions, then that is indeed the most trustworthy handhold (al-'Urwa al-Wuthqaa) with no break in it.

[But] whoever says with his tongue, but does not know with his Heart, and has not validated that with his Actions, then such would not be accepted from him, and he would be in the Hereafter from among the Losers."

Hilyat Al-Awliyaa 2/291

Hasan al Basri said:

"Do not purchase the love of a thousand men with the anger of one man."

Miftah Dar al-Sa'adah by ibn al Qayyim

Ibn Muflih said: "*As for innovation, then repentance from it is by affirming it, and to recant from it, and to believe in the opposite of what he believed previously…*" Then he said: "It has been narrated from Al-Marrūdhī that Ahmad Ibn Hanbal said:

"When a innovator repents, then leave him in that state for a year until his repentance is verified to be correct."

He used as a proof the narration of Ibrāhīm At-Taymī when the people differed with him concerning Sabīgh Ibn 'Asal (the innovator) when he warned from sitting with him. So after a year had passed, he said, "*Now you may sit with him but be cautious of him.*"

(See Al-Ādāb Ash-Sharī'ah, 1/137)

Musa ibn Mualla said Hudhaifah advised me:

"There are three qualities that if you have them, you will get a share of every good that comes from above: your deeds should be only for the sake of Allah, you should love for people what you love for yourself and your food should be lawful."

Sifatus-Safwah 4/269 by Ibn al Jawzi

Al Murrudi reported that he asked Imam Ahmad:

"How are you today?"

Imam Ahmad said:

"How can I be while I am required by my Lord to perform obligatory acts of worship, by my Prophet to practice my Sunnah, by the two angels to improve my deeds, and my soul urges to follow it, Satan pushes me to commit evil deeds, the angel of Death is waiting to take my life, and my children are asking me to provide for them?"

Siyar alam Nubalaa 11/227 by Adh Dhahabi

Ibn Uyaynah said Amr ibn al-As said:

"The wise one is not the one who knows good from evil, but he who knows the better of two evils."

Siyar alam Nubalaa 3/74 by Adh-Dhahabi

Abu al Mundhir Ismail ibn Umar said I have heard Abu Abdurrahman al Umari saying:

"The negligence of a person lies in his reluctance to obey Allah, when he sees something which displeases Allah, overlooks it and

does not enjoin good and forbid evil for fear of those who have no power to harm or help."

Sifatus Safwah 2/181 by ibn al jawzi

Ahmad ibn Isaam reported that Zuhair ibn Nuaim said:

"This religion will not be established without 2 things: Patience and Certainty. It will not be established only with certainty; neither will it be established with patience only. In fact, Abu ad-Darda has given an example for them and said: The likeness of patience and certainty is as the likeness of two farmers who dig up the soil, if one sits down, the other sits down too."

Sifatus Safwah 4/8 by ibn al jawzi

Abu Qasim ibn Manee' said:

"I wanted to go to Suwaid ibn Sa'eed, so I said to Ahmed ibn Hanbal to write to him [about me], so he wrote: And this [is a] man [who] writes (or records) Hadeeth.

So I said: Oh Abu Abdullah, [just or only that!] after all my years of service to you and after all the time I spent with you?! If only you wrote: This is a man from the People of Hadeeth.

So he said: A man of Hadeeth according to us is he who acts upon and uses the Hadeeth."

Manaqib al-Imam Ahmed by Ibn Al-Jawzi, p.208

Hasan al Basri said:

"If there is music involved in a dinner invitation (waleemah), do not accept the invitation."

Al-Jaami by al-Qayrawaani p.262-263

Abu Amr Al-Awzai said:

"We go with the Sunnah, wherever it goes."

Tareekh Ibn 'Asaakir 35/200

Ibnul-Qayyim stated: "*The source of shirk and its foundation that it returns back to is negation and it is of three categories:*

Negation of the created thing of its Maker and Creator [wherein the creation denies its Creator]

Negating the Maker [the Most Perfect, One who is free of all imperfections] of His perfection by negating His Names, His Attributes and His Actions.

Negation of conducting oneself with Him in a manner that is obligatory upon the servant from the true actualisation of Tawheed."

Al-Jawāb al-Kāfī (p. 299)

Ibn Abdil-Barr said:

"[Utilizing] difference of opinion is not a proof with any of the people of knowledge from the jurists of the Ummah, except for the one who has no insight, has no knowledge with him and has no proof for his saying."

Jāmi' Bayān al-'Ilm wa Fadhlihi, 2/229

al-Khattābi said:

"And differing is not a proof – rather the explanation of the Sunnah is a proof for those who differ with each other, from the earlier people and the later people."

A'lāmul-Hadeeth 3/2092

Imām Mālik Ibn Anas stated with regard to the Sahābah:

"There is not in the differing of the Sahābah an excuse (or allowance). Indeed there is only that which is wrong or right."

Jāmi' Bayānil-'Ilm wal-Fadlihi

Rabee' Ibn Hādi said:

"Indeed the Salafis are not infallible, however, they are the People upon the Truth (Ahlul-Haq), they are Ahlus-Sunnah and they are the best of people in 'Aqeedah, Manhaj, manners, etiquettes, and knowledge."

Majmū' Kutub wa Rasā'il wa Fatāwa of Shaikh Rabee',10/115

ibn Taymiyah said:

"And whoever his sins are plenty, then his greatest remedy is Jihad."

Majmou' Al-Fatawa 28/421

Ibn Kathīr said:,

"As for Ahlus-Sunnah wal-Jamā'ah, then they say about every action and saying that is not established from the Sahābah that it is an innovation (bid'ah). That is because if it had been something good, they would have preceded us with it due to the fact that there is not a single trait from the traits of goodness except that they hastened to it."

Tafsir Ibn Kathir 7278

Sa'eed Ibn Jubayr said:

"That my son should accompany a sinful highway robber who is a Sunnee is more beloved to me than him taking as his companion a worshipping innovator."

Mentioned by Ibn Battah in "Al-Ibaanatus-Sughraa", no. 132.

Ibn Taymiyyah said:

"Accordance to the Sunnah and Ijmaa' (consensus), Ahlul-Bid'ah are worse than the people of sinful desires and lusts. The sins of the people of disobedience involves doing that which is forbidden such as stealing or fornicating or drinking wine or consuming wealth falsely. The sins of the people of innovation involves abandoning that which Allaah has commanded which is following of the Sunnah and the Jamaa'ah of the believers."

See "Majmoo al-Fataawaa" 20/103.

Al-Imām Abu Muhammad Ibn Tamīm Al-Hanbalī said describing Imām Ahmad:

"He was harsh against ahlul-bid'ah and against the one who drew close to them if he did not abandon them, even if his 'aqīdah was correct."

Tabaqāt al-Hanābilah of Abu Ya'lā 2/289, Tahrīm an-Nadhr fī Kutubil-Kalām p.60

Ahmad (18524) narrated from al-Baraa' ibn 'Aazib, that the Messenger of Allah said:

"Indeed the strongest bond of faith is to love for the sake of Allah and hate for the sake of Allah."

Classed as hasan by the commentators on al-Musnad; also classed as hasan by al-Albaani in Saheeh at-Targheeb (3030).

In an authentic hadeeth collected by Imaam Ibn Hibbaan in his Saheeh (no.276), the Messenger of Allaah said:

"Whoever seeks the Pleasure of Allaah while angering the people will have Allaah pleased with him, who shall make the people pleased with him [anyway]. Whoever seeks to please the people while angering Allaah will have Allaah angry with him, who shall make the people angry with him [anyway]."

Abu Huraira reported Allah's Messenger as saying:

"He who called (people) to righteousness, there would be reward (assured) for him like the rewards of those who adhered to it, without their rewards being diminished in any respect. And he who called (people) to error, he shall have to carry (the burden) of its sin, like those who committed it, without their sins being diminished in any respect."

Sahih Muslim 2674

Narrated Hudhaifa bin Al-Yaman:

The people used to ask Allah's Messenger about the good but I used to ask him about the evil lest I should be overtaken by them. So I said, "O Allah's Messenger! We were living in ignorance and in an (extremely) worst atmosphere, then Allah brought to us this good (i.e., Islam); will there be any evil after this good?" He said, "Yes." I said, 'Will there be any good after that evil?" He replied, "Yes, but it will be tainted (not pure.)" I asked, "What will be its taint?" He replied, "(There will be) some people who will guide others not according to my tradition? You will approve of some of their deeds and disapprove of some others." I asked, "Will there be any evil after that good?" He replied, "Yes, (there will be) some people calling at the gates of the (Hell) Fire, and whoever will respond to their call, will be thrown by them into the (Hell) Fire." I said, "O Allah s Apostle! Will you describe them to us?" He said, "They will be from our own people and will speak our language." I said, "What do you order me to do if such a state should take place in my life?" He said, "Stick to the group of Muslims (Jamaah)and their Imam (ruler)." I said, "If there is neither a group of Muslims(Jamaah) nor an Imam (ruler)?" He said, "Then turn away from all those sects even if you were to bite (eat) the roots of a tree till death overtakes you while you are in that state."

Sahih Bukhari 7084

Narrated Abu Umayah Ash-Sha'bani:

"I went to Abu Tha'balah Al-Khushani and said to him: 'How do you deal with this Ayah?' He said: 'Which Ayah?' I said: 'Allah's saying: Take care of yourselves! If you follow the guidance no harm shall come to you (5:105).' He said: 'Well, by Allah! I asked one well-informed about it, I asked the Messenger of Allah about it. [So] he said: "Rather, comply with (and order) the good, and stay away from (and prohibit) the evil, until you see avarice obeyed, desires followed, and the world preferred, and everyone is amazed with his view. Then you should be worried about yourself in particular, and worry of the common folk. Ahead of

you are the days in which patience is like holding onto an ember, for the doer (of righteous deeds) during them is the like of the reward of fifty of those who do the like of what you do."
'Abdullah bin Al-Mubarak said*: "It was added for me, by other than 'Utbah, that it was said: 'O Messenger of Allah! The reward of fifty men among us, or them?' He said: 'No! Rather the reward of fifty men among you.'"*

Jami Tirmidhi Grade:Sahih English reference : Vol. 5, Book 44, Hadith 3058 Arabic reference : Book 47, Hadith 3335

Imam Al-Barbaharee said:

"Whoever hides sincere advice from the Muslims has acted deceitfully towards them so it is not permissible to hide sincere advice from any of the Muslims, whether pious or impious, in matters of the religion. Whoever hides that has acted deceitfully towards the Muslims. Whoever acts deceitfully towards the Muslims has done so towards the religion. Whoever acts deceitfully towards the religion has behaved treacherously towards Allah, His Messenger and the Believers."

Sharus-Sunnah by Imam Barbaharee

Abu Sa'id Al Khudri said:

"Allah's Messenger said, "If a person embraces Islam sincerely, then Allah shall forgive all his past sins, and after that starts the settlement of accounts, the reward of his good deeds will be ten times to seven hundred times for each good deed and one evil deed will be recorded as it is unless Allah forgives it.""

Sahih al-Bukhari 41

Abu Sa`id al-Khudri said:

"I heard the Messenger of Allah say, "Whosoever of you sees an evil, let him change it with his hand; and if he is not able to do so, then [let him change it] with his tongue; and if he is not able to do so, then with his heart — and that is the weakest of faith."

Sahih Muslim and 40 Hadith of Nawwawi

Jabir ibn Abdullah said:

The Prophet said: "If any man is among a people in whose midst he does acts of disobedience, and, though they are able to make him change (his acts), they do not change, Allah will smite them with punishment before they die."

Sunan Abi Dawud 4339 Grade: Hasan

Abu Hurairah narrated the Messenger of Allah said:

"Islam began as something strange and will go back to being strange, so glad tidings to the strangers.'"

Sunan Ibn Majah 3986 Grade: Sahih

Narrated Mu'awiyah:

"I heard the Messenger of Allah say: Migration(Hijra) will not end until repentance ends, and repentance will not end until the sun rises in the west."

Sunan Abi Dawud 2479 Grade: Sahih

Narrated Abu Umamah:

"The Prophet said: If anyone loves for Allah's sake, hates for Allah's sake, gives for Allah's sake and withholds for Allah's sake, he will have perfect faith."

Sunan abi Dawud 4681 Grade: Sahih

www.ingramcontent.com/pod-product-compliance
Lightning Source LLC
Chambersburg PA
CBHW071727120626
46550CB00002B/416
9781967724161